ISBN 3-89417-120-0

Bibliographic information published by Die Deutsche Bibliothek
detailed bibliographic data is available in the Internet at http://dnb.ddb.de.

© by Philippka-Sportverlag, D-48159 Münster
Editing: Konrad Honig, Ulrich Blennemann, Sean McAfee
Translations: Patrick Hubenthal
Production managing: Werner Böwing, Judith Rupprecht, Gudrun Quilling
Illustrations: Frauke Hehn, Marion Beckmann, Janet Rittig
Layout and Design: Thorsten Krybus, Marion Beckmann
Photos: Alfred Harder (page 3), others: firo sportphoto
Printing: Silber Druck, D-34266 Niestetal

THE COMPLETE 'KEEPER

Youth Goalkeeper Training from A to Z

by

Peter Greiber
and
Robert Freis

CONTENTS

1 **Goalkeeper Training** — **6**

Basic Principles — **10**
Organizing a Training Program — **12**

2 **Goalkeeper Techniques** — **14**

The Basic Position — **16**
Basic Position on Shots
Basic Position on Crosses
Balls on the Ground — **18**
Picking up Balls from the Front or Side
Diving and Landing
Low Balls in the Air — **20**
Catching Low Balls from the Front
Diving and Rolling Sideways
High Balls in the Air — **22**
Catching High Balls from the Front
Catching High Crosses
Deflecting and Punching Out — **24**
Low Balls in the Air and on the Ground
Deflecting High Balls
Punching out High Balls
Attack Building/Distribution — **26**
Rolling the Ball
Throwing the Ball
Kicking the Ball
Punting the Ball
Drop-Kicking the Ball

3 **Basic Goalkeeper Tactics** — **32**

Practicing Tactics — **35**
Basic Tactical Building Blocks — **36**
Positional Play on Various Types of Shots and Crosses — 36
Cooperating with Defenders on Corner Kicks — 40
Cooperating with Defenders on Free Kicks — 41
1 v. 1 Situations — 42
1 + 1 v. 1 and 1 + 1 v. 2 — 43
1 v. 1 in the Air — 50
Dealing with Back Passes — 51

4 **8- to 10-Year-Olds: Basic Ball Training** — **68**

A Few Guidelines for Working with 8- to 10-Year-Olds — **69**
Becoming a Goalkeeper (Coordination) — **70**

10- to 12-Year-Olds: The Start of Focused Training   78   5

Performance Profile   **80**
Technical Skills   **82**
Coordination: Running Exercises   **92**
Practical Exercises for Individual Techniques   **102**
     Catching Low and High Balls (from the Front or Side)   102
     Diving and Rolling Sideways on Ground Balls   110
     Throwing, Kicking, Punting, Drop-Kicking   114
Sample Practice Session   **118**

Moving On: Intermediate Training with 12- to 14-Year-Olds   122   6

Age-Appropriate Warm-Up Programs   **123**
Coordination: Running Exercises   **125**
Practice Games and Exercises   **130**
Teaching Technical Skills   **132**
     High Balls: Catching Shots from the Front and Side   134
     Diving and Rolling Sideways on Ground Balls   138
     Balls in the Air: Diving, Jumping and Rolling   142
     Deflection Techniques   146
     Throwing, Kicking, Punting, Drop-Kicking   150
     Field Player Skills: Receiving Back Passes   154
Sample Practice Session   **156**

The Finishing Touches: Advanced Training with 14- to 18-Year-Olds   160   7

Performance Profile   **162**
Age-Appropriate Warm-Up   **164**
Coordination and Technique: Running Exercises   **165**
Goalkeeper Techniques   **169**
     Catching High Balls from the Front and from the Side   170
     Diving and Rolling Sideways on Ground Balls   174
     Diving and Jumping for High and Low Balls and Rolling Sideways   178
     Jumping to Deflect High Balls and Falling Backwards   182
     Jumping and Deflecting (Punching Out)   186
     Throwing, Kicking, Punting, Drop-Kicking   190
Sample Practice Session   **194**

Equipment and Accessories   198   8

Goalkeeper gloves   **198**
The Rebound Net   **201**
     Goalkeeper Technique Exercises Using the Rebound Net   201

Goalkeeper Training

General Remarks

In soccer, as in other games, the importance of the goalkeeper cannot be overstated. The goalkeeper's performance is the deciding factor in many victories – and many defeats. And yet, specialized goalkeeper training seldom is incorporated into the regular practice sessions of most amateur or youth teams. This is due in part to the need for a quite different type of training from that required by field players. As a result, most top clubs have special goalkeeper coaches, who run a separate position-specific training program for their goalkeepers (either alone or together with other goalkeepers in the club). This type of training is specifically designed for the complex demands of the position, putting the keeper in realistic match-type situations as often as possible. Achieving this means goalkeepers must practice with field players during certain phases of the training program, participating in exercises that focus on both field play and goalkeeping. Certain individual and group tactics also require the goalkeeper to practice with the rest of the team.

Should goalkeeper training focus primarily on learning and perfecting goalkeeping techniques, or on conditional factors like strength, speed and endurance? This is a matter of some debate, but our experience suggests that it's better to teach goalkeeper-specific techniques and movement sequences than to put too much emphasis on condition, particularly with young goalkeepers.

However, even goalkeepers with perfect technique will have trouble reaching well-aimed shots if they can't get into position in time. So in addition to improving technique, goalkeeper coaches also need to pay some attention to training coordination and basic motor skills.

Naturally, the basic principles of soccer training apply to goalkeepers just as much as they do to field players. When you plan regular practice sessions, you take individual field players' strengths and weaknesses into account; you should do the same for your goalkeepers. Periods of intense exertion should alternate with rest periods for goalkeepers just as they do for field players. It makes more sense to work in terms of "small" series, make corrections as needed and give praise and encouragement than it does to kick 20 shots or more at a single goalkeeper in rapid succession. Ultimately, when it comes to the mental aspects of training, there's no real difference between goalkeepers and field players other than recognizing the special mental requirements of the position.

What to Teach, and When?

This question is just as important for goalkeepers as it is for field players. A good coach takes it into account always when planning training: What must be taught at a specific age level, what can be taught, and what exercises are applicable under all conditions?

The body parts involved in any given sequence of movements are controlled by commands from the central nervous system (CNS). The CNS initiates each individual movement, choosing from a vast repertoire of possible movements. The coordination of sensory organs, muscles and, for example, arms and legs, is what we call "psychomotor performance capacity," or more simply "motor ability." This term encompasses the coordination and control of movements, the adaptation of movements and movement

sequences to various situations (many of which are subject to rapid change) and, ultimately, the mastery of athletic techniques – in this case, goalkeeper-specific techniques. Motor ability and the factors influencing it (endurance, strength, speed, mobility and coordination) undergo a long process of growth and development. For optimal results, we can take advantage of this process by using different types of training at different age levels (for specific information, see the exercises and developmental principles in each chapter of this book).

It's well-known that young players are most easily trained during so-called "sensitive phases." In other words, during certain periods in the development of growing children, the conditions necessary for optimal athletic performance reach a natural peak. We will use these "sensitive phases" as guideposts as we discuss the best way to organize your youth training program, what to teach, and when.

Note: Although this book is intended primarily for coaches of youth soccer teams, many of the exercises (especially the ones for 14- to 18-year-olds) are appropriate for adults as well.

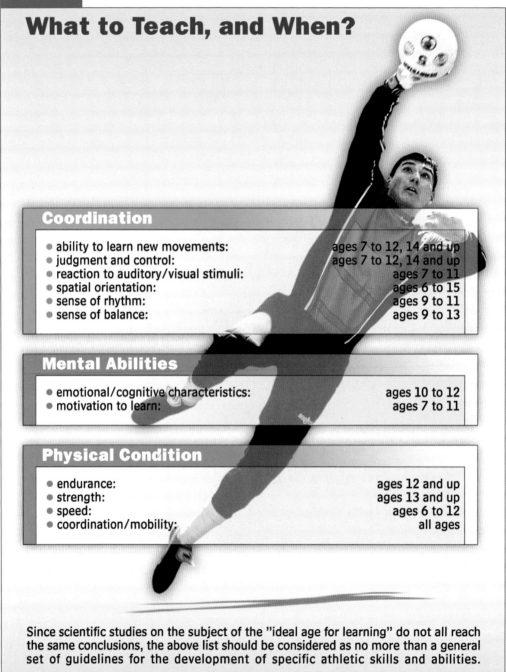

Illustr. 1

What to Teach, and When?

Coordination

- ability to learn new movements: ages 7 to 12, 14 and up
- judgment and control: ages 7 to 12, 14 and up
- reaction to auditory/visual stimuli: ages 7 to 11
- spatial orientation: ages 6 to 15
- sense of rhythm: ages 9 to 11
- sense of balance: ages 9 to 13

Mental Abilities

- emotional/cognitive characteristics: ages 10 to 12
- motivation to learn: ages 7 to 11

Physical Condition

- endurance: ages 12 and up
- strength: ages 13 and up
- speed: ages 6 to 12
- coordination/mobility: all ages

Since scientific studies on the subject of the "ideal age for learning" do not all reach the same conclusions, the above list should be considered as no more than a general set of guidelines for the development of specific athletic skills and abilities.

SIS MAGAZINE

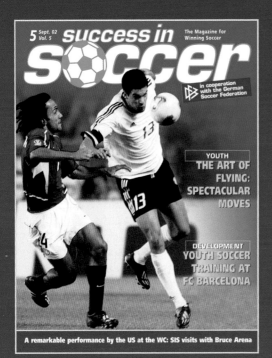

5 Sept. 02 Vol. 5

The Magazine for Winning Soccer

success in soccer

in cooperation with the German Soccer Federation

YOUTH
THE ART OF FLYING: SPECTACULAR MOVES

DEVELOPMENT
YOUTH SOCCER TRAINING AT FC BARCELONA

A remarkable performance by the US at the WC: SIS visits with Bruce Arena

SUCCESS IN SOCCER – (SIS) – a magzine dedicated exclusively to modern training methods.

SIS is the offspring of the successful magazine *fussballtraining*, a publication of the German Soccer Federation on effective soccer training since 1983.

SIS combines the latest information on techniques and tactics from Germany's top soccer minds with input from respected coaches from other countries, providing critical training support for soccer players at all levels – from youth leagues all the way up to the National Team.

SIS shows how to improve a team's game, with practical tips on specific subjects, including

▶ how to organize interesting and effective practice sessions,

▶ how to teach techniques and tactics the right way

▶ new tactics coaches can use in play and practice – and much more

With lots of diagrams and photos.

Basic Principles

Generell Remarks

Just like field players, goalkeepers should strive to improve their technical-tactical skills and physical abilities continuously at every age level. In the "performance profile" for each level, we've listed the techniques that goalkeepers should master before they reach the next level, so that they can continue to develop.

We've intentionally used the word "should" instead of "must," because it's completely normal for sudden "growth spurts" to be followed by periods of stagnation. Coaches have to be resourceful – sometimes a sympathetic educator, sometimes a tough drill instructor – but a continuous and clearly structured training program will always be effective in the long run.

The practical question of whether goalkeeper training should be incorporated into the team's regular practice sessions cannot be answered with a simple yes or no. In professional soccer, separate goalkeeper training is practically the rule (apart from team and group tactics training, which requires goalkeepers and field players to practice together). At lower levels and in youth soccer, separate goalkeeper training usually runs into a major obstacle: limitations on the coach's time. For many of these teams, a separate goalkeeper training session even once a week would be a major accomplishment. And at least some parts of the general training program – crosses from the outside forwards, 1 v. 1 situations in front of the goal, and similar exercises – do provide plenty of action for the goalkeepers.

If you want to be a big star, you have to start small!

Guidelines:

• The contents of each session (technique, tactics and condition) should be appropriate for players' age and ability level.
• The smaller the group, the more you can focus on the goalkeepers. The ideal size for technique training is two to four goalkeepers; for condition training, the group can be bigger.
• Make practice intense, focused, varied and interesting – from 60 to 80 minutes, depending on the age level.
• A rule of thumb: Always move from easy to hard, from simple to complex.
• Practice new techniques by themselves at first, and then gradually combine them.
• Always combine coordination training with goalkeeper-specific technique training.
• The warm-up and the main portion of each session should always focus on a specific concept.
• Use warm-up to prepare players for the main session's focus point.
• Use general discussions and individual corrections to address mistakes (focus on the major problems); offer simple solutions.

• Instead of long sets with lots of repetition, exercises should be short, intense and demand full concentration.
• Exercises should approximate actual match play.
• Goalkeepers need goals (even if they're just two cones) in every exercise, as clear points of reference and orientation.
• Include motivational exercises at the end of every practice session.
• It's a good idea for all goalkeepers to practice with other age levels; for example, 9- to 10-year-old goalkeepers should practice regularly with the 10- to 11-year-old team, whose goalkeepers should practice with the 11- to 12-year-olds, etc. (An advantage is that they become more comfortable playing with players who are older and physically more mature).

Group training with goalkeepers of different age levels is a great way to improve everyone's performance.

Organizing a Training Program

For players younger than 8 years old, separate goalkeeper training should definitely be avoided; otherwise they may start specializing too early.

Creating Practice Groups:

8- to 10-Year-Olds

- Younger and older players together: Two to four goalkeepers
- Frequency of practice: Twice per week before and during the regular session
- Session length: 45 to 60 minutes

10- to 12-Year-Olds

- Younger and older players together: Four goalkeepers (provided each team has two)
- Frequency of practice: Twice per week before and during the regular session
- Session length: 60 minutes

12- to 14-Year-Olds

- Younger and older players together: Four goalkeepers (provided each team has two)
- Frequency of practice: Twice per week before, during and independent of the regular session
- Session length: 60 to 70 minutes

Illustr. 2b

If the conditions for goalkeeper training in your club are less than ideal, consider unconventional solutions: Could you improve the situation by working with another club in the area? Ideas like these should not be taboo; in fact, coaches should actively promote them.

14- to 16-Year-Olds

• Younger and older players together:	Four goalkeepers (provided each team has two)
• Frequency of practice:	Three times per week before, during and independent of the regular session
• Session length:	70 to 90 minutes

16- to 18-Year-Olds

• Once per week with 15- to 16-year-olds and adults	Two to four goalkeepers
• Frequency of practice:	Three times per week before, during and independent of the regular session
• Session length:	70 to 90 minutes

Naturally, the concept presented above only makes sense if your club has the same number of youth teams, goalkeepers and coaches as shown here. Team makeup, frequency of practice and time available for separate goalkeeper training sessions also are factors.

Goalkeeper Techniques

You Can't Teach an Old Dog...

Good technique is one of the single most important prerequisites for a successful career as a goalkeeper. Therefore, a major objective of youth goalkeeper training is for players to execute the movement sequences involved in goalkeeping techniques as automatically as possible. Players who learn the wrong moves when they're young will have a very hard time correcting the problem later.

No goalkeeper will master all or even most goalkeeping techniques perfectly. Good coaches know how far they can push their goalkeepers, in terms of technical development, and when they have to make do with what they've already accomplished, for better or for worse.

In the following pages we present the techniques the goalkeeper executes with the ball. We review the basic elements of each technique in detail, as well as typical mistakes. Included among these techniques is the "basic" or "starting" position that the goalkeeper should assume before each play.

Appropriate exercises for teaching these techniques (and other movements with and without the ball) are presented in later chapters, arranged by age level.

In the section on "Deflecting and Punching Out," note that goalkeepers should generally try to catch or stop most balls and secure them against the body. During practice, shots should be aimed so that goalkeepers have a chance to catch them, especially in youth soccer. Punching out and deflecting should not become a part of your training program until your goalkeepers have mastered the catching techniques.

Here's how you do it: Take off strong, swing your arms and your other leg up (the leg provides good protection, too), catch the ball in front of you at the highest point possible and secure it against your body.

Basic Position on Shots

NOTES ON TECHNIQUE

- Place your feet shoulder-width apart and in line with your hips.
- Bend your knees slightly; place your weight on the balls of your feet.
- Bend forward slightly from the hips/waist.
- Hold your arms out to the sides, with elbows slightly bent and forward, hands open and palms facing toward the ball.
- Maintain sharp focus – don't let your body relax!
- Keep your eyes on the ball.

TIP

The position changes according to the distance between you and your opponent (and the ball): As a shooter gets closer to the goal, and the chance of the ball being chipped over you diminishes, make your stance more compact (lower to the ground).

Basic Position on Crosses

NOTES ON TECHNIQUE

- Stand in the rear third of the goal, with your back to the goal.
- Place your feet shoulder-width apart and in line with your hips.
- Bend your knees slightly; place your weight on the balls of your feet.
- Stay light on your feet and ready for action.
- Hold your arms next to your body, elbows bent and hands open.
- Maintain sharp focus.
- Keep your eyes on the ball.

TIP

The position described above is for crosses from the goal line/corner; on crosses from inside positions, there are two important differences: Face toward the ball and stand in front of the center of the goal.

TIP

By bending at the knees and hips, you lower your center of gravity.

COMMON PROBLEMS

- Feet are too close together.
- Upper body is too erect, arms hang loosely, hands are balled into fists.
- Knees are locked or bent too much.
- Back is hunched.
- Weight is too far back (on heels).

COMMON PROBLEMS

- Goalkeeper faces the ball directly (stance should be slightly diagonal).
- Goalkeeper stands in the front third of the goal.
- Feet are too close together.
- Back is hunched, arms hang loosely and/or hands are balled into fists.
- Knees are locked or bent too much.
- Weight is too far back (on heels).

Collecting Balls from the Front or Side

NOTES ON TECHNIQUE

- Take a long stride behind the ball, then close the gap between your front and rear feet by lowering your rear knee; ideally, though, the knee should not touch the ground (to keep the game moving quickly).
- Place your weight on the balls of your feet.
- If the ball is headed to your right, bring your right foot forward (same on the left).
- Stretch your arms toward the ball, open your hands, and keep your elbows as close together as possible.
- At the moment of impact, let your arms move back toward your body somewhat to absorb the ball's momentum.
- To keep the game moving quickly, always try to scoop up the ball while moving forward.

Diving and Landing (Sideways)

NOTES ON TECHNIQUE

- The object is to get on the ground and behind the ball quickly; hips, upper body and arms all go sideways and down simultaneously.
- Keep your elbows in front of your body.
- Roll across your hips, side and shoulder.
- Stop the ball in front of you: On a ball headed to your right, take a quick step toward the ball with your right foot (this shifts your weight onto that foot), drop quickly (driving with the opposite leg/knee) and get your upper body behind the ball.

- Get your hands behind the ball.
- The bottom hand should be below the midline of the ball, the top hand above it.
- Keep your eyes on the ball.
- Balance: If you dive onto your right side, drive your left knee forward somewhat (toward your chest) to keep from rolling onto your back. If you fall onto your left side, bring your right knee forward.
- Secure the ball against your body.

COMMON PROBLEMS
- Goalkeeper squats, feet and knees are too far apart.
- Goalkeeper stops beside the ball, not behind it.
- Arms and hands "wait" for the ball instead of reaching for it.
- Both knees are on the ground.
- Hands reach down from above the ball.
- Front knee is between arms.
- Goalkeeper "sits" on rear leg.
- Goalkeeper stands up before securing the ball.

Photos read from right to left

COMMON PROBLEMS
- Instead of stepping toward the ball, goalkeeper simply falls sideways.
- Goalkeeper stops the ball while diving backwards.
- Upper body is too erect, arms extend forward.
- Goalkeeper stops watching the ball.
- Hands are not behind the ball.
- Hands slap at the ball.
- Goalkeeper lands on stomach (poor technique)
- Goalkeeper rolls backwards after landing (poor balance).

Catching Low Balls from the Front

NOTES ON TECHNIQUE

- Spread your legs slightly, move toward the ball.
- Bend forward slightly from the waist, but stay behind the ball.
- Extend your arms and hands to receive the ball.
- Keep your elbows as close together as possible.
- Your hands and upper arms should make the first contact with the ball (they absorb its momentum).
- Bend your upper body over the ball and wrap your hands around it.

Diving and Rolling Sideways

NOTES ON TECHNIQUE

- Take one or more steps to the side; on the last step, take a longer stride (the power step) and move diagonally forward ("step – power step – jump").
- Bend, then straighten the takeoff leg (here, the right leg); drive the other knee up high for added power and swing the arms all the way through.
- Shift your weight onto the takeoff leg.
- Move explosively with the takeoff leg (make contact briefly with the ground).
- Accelerate in a straight line toward the ball.
- Dive fast and move straight toward the ball.
- While you're in the air, catch the ball and secure it against your body.
- Absorb the impact by landing on your upper arm, shoulder and hip; or roll onto your stomach to control the momentum of your upper body.

COMMON PROBLEMS

- Instead of hands and arms, the chest makes the first contact with the ball.
- Goalkeeper stands too erect, placing the upper body between the ball and the goal.
- Goalkeeper steps or moves backwards (often with a small hop) instead of toward the ball.

Photos read from right to left

COMMON PROBLEMS

- Goalkeeper doesn't step toward the ball or take off with enough power.
- Goalkeeper jumps in an arc or takes off with both legs.
- Goalkeeper doesn't pull the ball in to the body and loses it upon landing.
- Goalkeeper lands on elbow.
- Goalkeeper doesn't bend the takeoff leg sufficiently or straighten it completely.
- Goalkeeper bends the takeoff leg too much; center of gravity is too low.

Catching High Balls from the Front

NOTES ON TECHNIQUE

- Catch the ball in front of your face and as soon as possible, at the highest point possible; the ankle, knee and hip of the takeoff leg should be fully extended.
- As you take off, swing the other knee up for extra power/protection.
- Get a running start: Wait first, then move toward the ball and jump.
- Keep your eyes on the ball.
- Swing your arms while you run and jump.
- Stretch your arms up toward the ball.
- Keep your wrists stiff and catch the ball with your fingers spread wide (thumbs behind the ball and pointing inward).
- Upon making contact with the ball, bend your elbows and pull the ball in to your body with both hands.
- Always take off with one leg, even in tight situations.

Catching High Crosses

NOTES ON TECHNIQUE

- Take quick, short steps to meet the ball.
- Make the last step (takeoff/power step) a long stride.
- Take off with the leg closer to the ball: If the ball is coming from the right, take off with the right leg (same on the left). The takeoff leg should be fully extended through ankle, knee and hip.
- Swing your arms while you run and jump.
- Swing the other knee (protection) and both arms up for a powerful takeoff.
- Catch the ball in front of your face, at the highest point possible, and secure it against your body.
- Land on the takeoff leg.
- Move decisively toward the ball.

COMMON PROBLEMS
- Goalkeeper stops watching the ball, catches it directly above or behind the head (instead of in front).
- Arms move up from the sides in an arc toward the ball, hands and thumbs are not behind the ball.
- Arms are not extended, goalkeeper catches the ball too late.
- Goalkeeper pulls the ball in too fast and carelessly, possibly losing it.
- Goalkeeper takes off with both legs.

COMMON PROBLEMS
- Goalkeeper takes off with both legs.
- Goalkeeper always takes off with the same leg, regardless of where the ball is coming from.
- Steps toward the ball are too long.
- Goalkeeper fails to drive the other knee up or jump for the ball.
- Goalkeeper bends the other knee but then straightens it again immediately, which pulls the body back down.
- Goalkeeper catches the ball in front of the chest or overhead.
- Goalkeeper catches the ball overhead without watching it.
- Goalkeeper lands on both feet or on the wrong foot.

Low Balls in the Air and on the Ground

NOTES ON TECHNIQUE
- Use the heel of the hand to deflect.
- Keep your wrist stiff.
- Thrust forward from the elbow to hit the ball.
- Deflect the ball as soon as possible.
- Deflect to the side, preferably out of the field.

TIP
In principle, goalkeepers should catch and secure every ball. During practice, shots should be aimed so that goalkeepers can catch them, especially in youth soccer. Punching out and deflecting should not become a part of your training program until your goalkeepers have mastered the catching techniques.

Deflecting High Balls

NOTES ON TECHNIQUE
- Keep your eyes on the ball.
- Take a quick step sideways before you jump to meet the ball.
- Make the last step a big one.
- If you're taking off with the left leg, reach overhead with your right arm and knock the ball over or beside the goal (depending on where it's coming from).
- If you're taking off with the right leg, reach overhead with your left arm to deflect the ball.
- Use your fingertips (one hand only!) to knock the ball over or beside the goal.
- Deflect to a teammate or out of touch.

COMMON PROBLEMS
- Goalkeeper uses the fingers to deflect.
- Wrist is loose.
- Instead of thrusting the arm forward, the goal-keeper simply extends it to meet the ball.
- Arm swings forward to slap the ball.
- Goalkeeper knocks the ball back onto the field.

COMMON PROBLEMS
- Goalkeeper takes off with the wrong leg.
- Instead of reaching overhead, goalkeeper reaches for the ball with the wrong arm.
- Goalkeeper knocks the ball back onto the field.
- Goalkeeper does not jump directly toward the ball.
- Goalkeeper does not hit the ball at the highest point possible.
- Body turns too soon, i.e. goalkeeper jumps "face-down."

Punching out High Balls

NOTES ON TECHNIQUE

- Before punching out, observe your surroundings, teammates and opponents, then focus on the ball.
- Ball both hands into fists.
- Get a running start: Wait first, then move toward the ball and jump.
- Two-handed punching out: Take off with the leg closer to the ball.
- One-handed punching out: If the ball is coming from the right, take off with the left leg, and vice versa.
- Swing the other knee (blocking) and both arms up for a powerful takeoff.
- Straighten the elbow quickly but not fully; move the arm diagonally to meet the ball squarely at the highest point possible.
- Punch with the hand that's closer to the ball and try to knock it to the opposite side.

Distributing the Ball: Rolling

NOTES ON TECHNIQUE

- Clamp the ball between hand and forearm; extend your other arm horizontally forward, keeping it loose.
- With the leg that's farther away from the ball, take a lunge step in the direction you want to roll it, simultaneously pulling the ball back alongside your body.
- Bend the forward knee and lean forward slightly from the waist.
- Roll the ball flat along the ground; keep your hand on it as long as possible and "point" in the direction of the roll.

COMMON PROBLEMS

- Goalkeeper glances away from ball.
- Goalkeeper takes off with both legs, without getting a running start.
- Hand starts too low and has to travel too far.
- Hand is not balled into a fist, goalkeeper slaps with an open hand.
- Goalkeeper does not straighten elbow.
- Fist hits ball off center.
- Goalkeeper punches with the hand that's farther away from the ball.
- Goalkeeper punches the ball back the way it came.
- Goalkeeper concentrates more on opponents than on the ball.

TIP

- Rolling the ball is good for covering short distances, as long as there aren't any opponents between goalkeeper and receiver.

COMMON PROBLEMS

- Goalkeeper rolls the ball too soon or too late.
- Goalkeeper throws the ball from the hip.
- Hand "points" sideways, not in the direction of the roll.
- Goalkeeper doesn't step in the direction of the roll, or rolls while running.

Distributing the Ball: Throwing

NOTES ON TECHNIQUE

- Using both hands, bring the ball back past your body and extend your throwing arm, clamping the ball between hand and forearm and letting your head and upper body follow the turn (eyes on the ball).
- With the leg that's farther away from the ball, take a step in the direction you're going to throw.
- "Open" your upper body by bringing your other arm quickly forward; the throwing arm follows immediately.
- Keep your hand on (and preferably behind) the ball as long as possible; otherwise you lose too much power.
- Throw the ball either sidearm or overhead; the rear leg follows the throw (follow through).

Goal kicks

NOTES ON TECHNIQUE

- Run up diagonally from behind.
- When you kick the ball, your other leg should be beside or slightly behind it.
- Kick the ball squarely in the center.
- Let your kicking leg swing through the ball (follow through).

TIPS

- The goalkeeper should always be the one to kick the ball. If another player kicks, that takes away a possible receiver and makes it impossible to force the opposition offsides.
- Set the ball in front of the goal: That way, if the kick is poor, you're not stuck outside of the goal.

COMMON PROBLEMS

- Goalkeeper faces direction of throw (stance should be sideways).
- Goalkeeper throws too soon, too late, or with a straight arm.
- Goalkeeper puts wrong foot forward.
- Upper body leans to one side.

COMMON PROBLEMS

- Plant leg is too far behind the ball, or even in front of it.
- Approach is not diagonal.
- Goalkeeper doesn't pull kicking leg back far enough before the kick.
- Poor follow through.
- Goalkeeper doesn't make solid contact with center of the ball.

Punting the Ball

NOTES ON TECHNIQUE
- Hold the ball in front of you with both arms extended.
- Take a few steps, then toss the ball ahead of you (young goalkeepers should use both hands for this).
- Kick the ball with the full instep.
- Swing the kicking leg all the way through the kick and down again, all in one fluid movement.

TIP
- The drop-kick (see below) is the fastest way to get the ball to a teammate. However, since drop-kicking is quite demanding technically, it's a good idea to start out with punting.

The Drop-Kick

NOTES ON TECHNIQUE
- Extend both arms and drop the ball in front of your body, or throw it up in the air with one hand.
- Kick the ball just after it bounces, while it's moving upward but before it reaches knee level (see Photo 2).
- The kick should be quick and short; the kicking leg moves only a short distance forward and then back again.
- Keep your ankle stiff and your toes pointing downward (kick the ball with the full instep).
- Plant your other foot next to the ball and point it in the direction of the kick.
- Depending on whether you want to kick the ball high, low, or on the ground, your upper body should lean either forward (for a kick on the ground) or back.

COMMON PROBLEMS
- Goalkeeper throws the ball too close to the body.
- Goalkeeper throws the ball to the side or too high.
- Upper body leans too far forward over the ball.
- Kicking leg swings sideways instead of straight toward the ball.
- Goalkeeper fails to make contact with the full instep, makes contact too late, or kicks the side of the ball.
- Poor follow-through: After the kick, the goalkeeper steps back instead of forward, usually because the upper body is leaning backwards.

COMMON PROBLEMS
- Goalkeeper throws the ball too high or drops it to one side.
- Goalkeeper kicks the ball too early or too late (usually with the shin).
- Goalkeeper allows the ball to bounce above knee level.
- Kicking motion is not quick and short.
- Ankle is loose.
- "Turned-in" foot: Goalkeeper kicks with the outside of the foot, and the ball goes sideways.

Basic Goalkeeper Tactics

Notes on Tactics Training for Goalkeepers

Tactics training is essential, not only for goalkeepers, but for the whole team.

Match analyses have shown that goalkeepers are only really put to the test four or five times per game. However, each such test can decide the entire match, and often these situations follow long periods when the keeper isn't directly involved in the action. So does this mean that goalkeepers are idle most of the time? Definitely not!

Goalkeepers are never idle; they have to stay focused and be ready to take an active role in the game at any time. Many dangerous situations can be nipped in the bud by an active, aware goalkeeper. The goalkeeper's duties also include organizing and directing the defense.

Over the course of a match, goalkeepers must adapt to every type of situation. The basis of this adaptability is "positional play," i.e. the goalkeeper's position in relation to the ball, teammates and opponents. If you want to improve your goalkeepers' tactics in a way that's truly systematic and relevant to match play, you have to have some combined practice sessions, with goalkeepers and field players together. This is the only way to create realistic game situations and tactical challenges for your goalkeepers.

OBJECTIVE OF TACTICS TRAINING:

The primary goal is to develop and improve a sense of the game as a whole and an ability to anticipate developments and situations.

GROUND RULES FOR TACTICAL PLAY:

Goalkeepers should watch the game at all times. Skilled positional play enables them to resolve situations to their advantage. They should get involved as early as possible.

Illustr. 3

Tactical Performance Profile

Goalkeeping can be divided into attacking and defensive plays, although most plays are actually a combination of the two. Example: Intercepting a cross, then distributing the ball.

Defensive Plays

- picking up the ball
- intercepting crosses and through-passes
- saving shots and headers
- 1 v. 1 challenges to win the ball
- receiving back passes

Attacking Plays

- throwing the ball
- kicking the ball
- punting the ball
- drop-kicking the ball
- participating in attack-building after back passes

Factors Affecting Performance

- goalkeeper-specific technical skills
- goalkeeper-specific field player techniques
- teammates' technical skills
- goalkeeper's positional play without the ball
- goalkeeper's positional play with the ball
- positions of teammates with and without the ball
- positions of opponents with and without the ball
- score
- weather, field, etc.

Attack-Building Plays: A Comparison

Kicking the Ball

When? To cover a short distance with a low pass (in the air or on the ground) to a teammate.
To cover a longer distance with a high pass to a teammate.

⊕ Good when the wind is at your back.

⊖ Hard for teammates to receive, since opponents occupy better positions. The longer the pass, the sooner opponents can start applying pressure.

Punting the Ball

When? To cover long distances.

⊕ Gains time when opponents are threatening the goal.
Good when the wind is at your back.
Good variation after multiple short passes.
Good if the opponents covering your forwards have poor heading skills.

⊖ Hard to aim and hard for teammates to receive, since opponents occupy better positions.

Throwing the Ball

When? To cover short and medium distances.

⊕ Accurate and easy for teammates to receive.

⊖ When used over longer distances, easy for opponents to press.

Drop-kicking the Ball

When? To cover any distance quickly.

⊕ Accurate and easy to receive due to the low arc.
Faster than kicking or punting.
Good when opponents are moving in after a corner kick or counterattack.
Good for a precise pass to a fast teammate.
Good when the opposition is pressing deep and aggressively.
Good when the wind is from the side.

⊖ Technically quite demanding for the goalkeeper, especially when field conditions are bad.

Practicing Tactics

1. Goalkeeper-specific tactics training can only be effective when field players (active team-mates and opponents) are involved.
2. The ability to deal with situations appropriately (this includes tactics) depends on a mastery of goalkeeper-specific techniques.

In practice, these two aspects of training must always be considered in relation to one another. The "Sample Exercises" shown for each technique make this clear. Many of these exercises (especially those involving a goal and multiple goalkeepers) combine tactical patterns with one or more goalkeeper techniques.

Separate goalkeeper technique training sessions don't accomplish much by themselves. It's the ability to apply skills to match situations that truly makes a good goalkeeper.

Simulating match play with opponents makes practice not only more interesting, but also more effective.

Basic Tactical Building Blocks

Positional Play on Various Types of Shots

The basic position is the goalkeeper's starting point for every play. However, there's not just one basic position; there are variations, depending on the situation, the distance between ball and goal, etc. (see also Chapter 2, "Goalkeeper Techniques"). We differentiate between two basic positions for two basic situations:
1. shots
2. crosses

A few important points:
• The basic position ultimately determines what actions a goalkeeper can take.
• It always depends on the position of the ball.
• The basic position is always preceded by a "bounce" and a preliminary step.
• The "bounce" (actually a small step forward) tenses the thigh muscles, enabling the goalkeeper to act quickly.
• The preliminary step also varies according to the position of the ball.

Mid- and Long-Range Shots

• Stand on an imaginary line between the ball and the center of the goal, out from the line but close enough to prevent being scored on by a high ball or chip.
• Take your preliminary step and assume the basic position just as the shooter winds up to shoot.
• Take a big step, since you have a relatively large amount of time.
• Bend your knees and hips slightly.
• Keep your arms in front of or beside your body.

• Hold your hands out to the sides, palms open.

Close-Range Frontal Shots

• Stand on an imaginary line between the ball and the center of the goal.
• Move as far forward as possible, to cut down the angle and take away more of the goal.
• Take a quick preliminary step and assume the basic position just as the shooter winds up.
• Bend your knees and hips a lot (envision a coiled spring).
• Hold your arms beside your body.
• You can drop your hands, since a chip over your head is practically impossible.
• Keep your eyes on the ball!
• You can dive forward or sideways to meet the ball, but never backwards.

Close-Range Diagonal Shots

The procedure here is similar to the one for frontal shots.
• Assume the basic position just as the shooter shoots.
• Bend your knees and hips, and bend forward slightly at the waist so as to present the biggest „target" possible.
• Always move forward to meet the ball.

Note:

Frontal and diagonal shots from various distances can be incorporated into almost any exercise, but be sure to keep things fresh (shots after dribbling, after passes, after combination plays). This forces goalkeepers to constantly adapt to new situations.

Positional Play on Various Types of Crosses

In Chapter 2, "Goalkeeper Techniques," we discussed the technical aspects of catching high balls from the front and from the side. Goalkeeping tactics related to 1 v. 1 situations in the air are covered on page 50.

General Notes on Tactics for Crosses

- As in other situations, successful goalkeeping on crosses depends on good positional play.
- Assume the basic position just as the ball leaves the crosser's foot.
- Now you have to decide whether to stay in the goal or run out (either way, let your teammates know what you're doing).
- Keep your arms in front of or beside your body.
- If you run out, take quick, short steps and run straight to a spot where you can intercept the ball.
- When intercepting crosses, keep your muscles flexed, to prepare yourself for physical contact with opponents. Protect yourself!
- Take one last long stride and take off powerfully toward the ball.
- Jump to meet the ball and catch it at the highest point possible.

Goalkeeper's Position on Crosses from the Goal Line

- Stand in the rear, middle or front third of the goal, depending on the crosser's position (distance from goal).
- Your stance should be almost parallel to the goal line, with your back to the goal.

... on Crosses from the Sideline

- Stand in the rear third or in the center of the goal.
- Turn slightly toward the ball.
- Stand farther away from the goal than you do on crosses from the goal line.

... on Crosses from Inside Positions

You should stand:
- in front of the goal, approximately in the center,
- facing the ball,
- either on the goal line or a few steps in front of it, depending on the crosser's position (the closer the crosser, the closer to the goal line).

... on Frontal Crosses

You should stand:
- in the middle of the goal,
- facing the ball,
- as far out in front of the goal as possible, depending on the crosser's position (but be sure the ball can't be chipped over your head).

Cooperating with Defenders on Corner Kicks

On corner kicks and free kicks, the goalkeeper has the primary responsibility for organizing the defensive line quickly and decisively, based on the roles assigned to each player by the coach.

Goalkeeper's Responsibilities

- Give quick and focused instructions to teammates.
- Quickly assign one defender to each goalpost. Both posts should always be covered by defenders specifically assigned to this job.
- Quickly assign your teammates to mark opponents in the immediate vicinity of the goal (be sure to pair them according to size, if the players haven't done this themselves already).
- Next, assign teammates to opponents farther away from the goal.
- Communicate with the player at the near post as necessary (this player is responsible for clearing any low shots in the air or on the ground that are aimed at the near post).

Goalkeeper's Actions

- Stand in the middle of the goal, facing the shooter rather than the midfield.
- As the soon as the ball moves, you have to decide whether to leave the goal, either to intercept or to clear the ball. Tell your teammates immediately what you're going to do ("Keeper!").
You should only move out from the goal if the shooter is extremely close (inside the goal box). Due to the large number of players in front of the goal, there's a high risk that teammates or opponents could get in your way if you leave the goal line.
- Shots aimed at the near post present the greatest danger, since they can be very

hard to reach if they get passed on toward the goal. Therefore, you should always try to prevent these shots from being passed on, either by yourself or together with your defenders.
- On short corner shots, your job is to direct the defensive line to move in on the ball.
- Take decisive action!

Cooperating with Defenders on Free Kicks

Goalkeeper's Responsibilities

- Give quick and focused instructions to teammates.
- Decide how many defenders should be involved in the wall.
- Quickly direct the defenders who will be involved in forming a wall.
- The second player in the wall should stand on an imaginary line between the ball and the goal posts, in order to protect the far corner of the goal (the one you're not standing in) from low shots on the ground and in the air.
- Quickly assign your teammates to opponents in the immediate vicinity of the goal.

Goalkeeper's Actions

- You should be right next to the wall. Choose a corner of the goal and stand in it (not in the center of the goal), and position the wall accordingly.
  - Stand either just in front of the goal line or a few steps farther out, depending on the position of the ball.
    - Do not leave your corner, not even for a moment, until you can tell where the ball is going.
      - Try to intercept the ball or clear it to the side.
        - If the wall blocks the shot, move as quickly as possible to your new position (determined by the position of the ball).

  Important: Stay focused! After blocking a free kick, defenders are very likely to assume — incorrectly — that the situation has been defused. Therefore:

- Immediately direct your full attention to the ball.
- If it comes toward the goal, take action!

1 v. 1 Situations

1 v. 1 against a Forward:

Contrary to what you might expect, goalkeepers and forwards have roughly equal chances of success when the attacker tries to dribble around the keeper. Therefore, you should always try to confront forwards directly and force them into 1 v. 1 situations, rather than letting them kick the ball past you or over your head. You should:

- get as close to the forward as possible without allowing the forward to chip you or shoot past you.
- close fast and decisively on the ball if the forward lets it get too far in front of him.
- move in quickly at first, then carefully.
- force your opponent to slow down and try to dribble around you.

In Every 1 v. 1 Situation:

- Assume a crouching position, but don't drop your buttocks too low.
- Stay loose and bend your knees and hips a lot, to shift your weight forward.
- Keep your stance fairly wide, so that you can move easily in any direction.
- To keep the ball from getting past you, stretch your arms past your thighs toward the ground and keep your palms open and facing forward.
- Concentrate on the ball; don't let the forward fool you with a body fake.
- Be patient; wait for the forward to make a move and then react.
- If the forward leaves the ball open, dive for it immediately.
- You can dive forward or sideways for the ball, but never backwards.
- If you do dive, make sure you can win or block the ball — a goalkeeper on the ground is helpless!

Try to delay the attacker long enough for your teammates to move up and either win the ball or force the forward away from the goal, preventing a controlled shot.

In practice, the coach and field players should recreate typical starting positions so the goalkeeper can experience this important situation.

1 + 1 v. 1 and 1 + 1 v. 2

1 + 1 v. 1

Basically, there are two versions of the situation "goalkeeper plus defender versus one attacker":

1. Forward dribbles toward defender.

Here, you should wait in front of the goal to see if your defender can win the ball. Move toward the ball cautiously, so you won't be surprised by any sudden shots or chips, and stop whenever the attacker touches the ball. You're waiting for the attacker to kick the ball too far ahead so you can make a quick, bold move to win or block it. If you're going to go for the ball, let your teammate know. That way your teammate can run behind you and protect the goal.

Note: You can practice for this situation with almost any exercise that's designed to improve individual tactics (attack and defense) for 1 v. 1 play.

2. Forward dribbles toward goalkeeper, followed by defender.

The primary difference between this situation and a 1 v. 1 with no defender is that the attacker is under time pressure (the defender is closing in from the rear). The attacker has a small head start but has to make a decision quickly in order to take advantage of it.
The defense has an excellent chance to defuse this situation if you can delay the attacker long enough for your defender to arrive.

You should use the same tactics described under Situation 1. While you try to block or stop the attacker, the defender should either help you or get behind you as quickly as possible and protect the goal.

Sample Exercises

EXERCISE 1

Two players (A and B) stand about 20 yards in front of a standard goal with goalkeeper. Attacker A stands facing the goal, legs apart, two yards in front of the coach (C, with ball). Defender B stands two yards behind the coach. C kicks the ball between A's legs, and A immediately runs after it. At the same time, B starts moving past C toward the goal. A tries to dribble around the goalkeeper and shoot, and B tries to prevent the shot.

FOCUS ON
- cooperation between goalkeeper and defender
- stopping the attacker

VARIATIONS
1. A can take any kind of shot.
2. A and B stand in front of the goal, but off to one side (left or right).
3. After winning the ball, B can counterattack on a 5-yard-wide goal (or a pair of cones, or a line), and A becomes the defender.
4. C throws the ball in an arc over A's head.
5. A stands in front of C, facing away from the goal. When C kicks the ball between A's legs, A has to turn around quickly and start after the ball.

EXERCISE 2

Attacker A and Defender B stand facing the goal, about four yards apart. The coach (C, with ball) stands three yards in front of A. C and A pass directly back and forth on the ground. At C's signal, A dribbles toward the goal and tries to shoot. B tries to prevent the shot.

FOCUS ON
- see Exercise 1

VARIATIONS
1. A can take any kind of shot.
2. A and B stand in front of the goal, but off to one side (left or right).
3. After winning the ball, B can counterattack on a 5-yard-wide goal (or a pair of cones, or a line), and A becomes the defender.
4. C throws the ball to A and A volleys back (alternating between the left foot and the right). At C's signal, A starts dribbling and the exercise proceeds as above.

EXERCISE 3

The coach (C) stands between two small goals (each three yards wide). C kicks the ball toward either the left or the right goal. A runs through that goal to the ball and then on toward the big goal (with goalkeeper). B has to run through the other goal before going after A.

FOCUS ON
• see Exercise 1

VARIATIONS

1. Players start from different starting positions (e.g. lying face down, push-up position, etc.).
2. Players have to execute various coordination exercises (e.g. forward or backward roll, spin in place) before going after the ball.

EXERCISE 4

Player A stands three yards in front of one small goal, Player B three yards in front of the other. In the center of each goal is a ball. The coach (C) calls out a name (either "A" or "B"), and both players run through "their" goals toward the big goal (with goalkeeper). The player whose name was called becomes the attacker and dribbles the ball from the small goal.

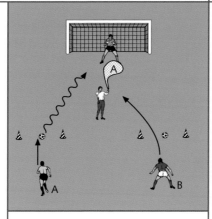

FOCUS ON
• see Exercise 1

VARIATIONS

1. The player whose name is called becomes the defender.
2. C uses hand signals to indicate who will be the attacker.
3. An extra cone stands two yards behind each player; both players have to run around these cones backwards before heading for the small goal.
4. At C's signal, the attacker gets the ball and passes it to C, who kicks a wall pass back into the attacker's path. The attacker receives the ball and dribbles to the goal.

Through Pass to a Forward

Forward versus Defender and Goalkeeper

On every pass, you have to judge whether the defender is in a position to stop the receiver (facing away from the goal).
Initially there is no danger of a shot or break-away. Assume a ready position a few yards in front of the goal and pay close attention to the 1 v. 1 as it develops, and also to the rest of the nearby action, ready to get involved at any moment. Change your position to follow the attacker and defender as they move.

Can the attacker receive the pass and turn toward the goal, creating a face-to-face 1 v. 1 situation? (see the exercises on the previous pages)

The closer the attacker gets to the goal, the greater the danger of a shot, so you should move into more of a crouching position (bent knees) and watch for the attacker to kick the ball past the defender toward the goal. You should also move back toward the

goal and be prepared for a sudden shot or chip.

Can the attacker receive the pass, turn toward the goal and shoot immediately?

Take a step toward the attacker and assume the basic position so you're ready for a shot. If the attacker doesn't shoot right away, try to move in closer.

Have you chosen a position that allows you to intercept a through pass?

To control the largest area possible, take a position somewhat farther away from the goal, but be sure the attacker can't chip the ball over your head. Move into a crouching position (bent knees) so you can move toward a through pass immediately.
If the attacker kicks a through pass, you have to decide immediately whether to go for it. This decision depends on the speed and direction of the pass, as well as the positions of your teammates and opponents. If the attacker moves closer to the goal instead of passing, move diagonally backwards toward the goal, taking quick, short steps. Stop whenever the attacker touches the ball.

Wait for the right moment and go for it!

Sample Exercises

EXERCISE 1

Using cones, mark out a 16 x 10-yard field just outside the penalty box. A defender stands on the left sideline, Attacker A on the right sideline. Attacker B has a ball and stands outside the field and between the other two players, at a cone 35 yards in front of the goal. A starts the exercise with a short showing run to receive the ball from B. The defender moves onto the field immediately and tries to stop A and prevent a shot and/or breakaway on goal.

FOCUS ON

- paying attention to the 1 v. 1
- preparing for a shot
- intercepting a possible through pass

VARIATIONS

1. The defender stands on the penalty box line directly in front of the goal and moves from there onto the field.
2. The defender stands at a cone directly behind A and moves onto the field as soon as A starts moving.
3. A has to pass back to B the first time and then show for another pass.

EXERCISE 2

Using cones, mark out a 16 x 10-yard field just outside the penalty box. A defender (with ball) stands on the left sideline, Attacker A on the right sideline. Attacker B stands outside the field and between the other two players, at a cone 35 yards in front of the goal. The defender passes on the ground to B. This pass is the starting signal for A, who immediately moves onto the field and shows for a pass on the ground from B. Then A heads for the goal; B tries to stop A and prevent a shot.

FOCUS ON

- see Exercise 1

VARIATIONS

1. The defender stands on the penalty box line directly in front of the goal and passes to Attacker B from there.
2. The defender stands at a cone behind A and passes from there to B.

EXERCISE 3

Using cones, mark out a 16 x 10-yard field just outside the penalty box. A defender stands on the right sideline where it meets the penalty box line, Attacker A on the left sideline. Attacker B has a ball and stands outside the field and between the other two players. A starts the exercise with a short showing run to receive a pass on the ground from B. As soon as A starts moving, the defender moves onto the field as well.

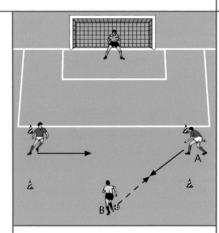

FOCUS ON
• see Exercise 1

VARIATIONS

1. Both players start from different starting positions (e.g. lying face down, lying face up, etc.).
2. Player A starts with a coordination exercise (e.g. forward roll), which the defender has to imitate before moving onto the field.
3. The defender stands behind A and cannot move onto the field until B passes the ball.

Grab the ball and secure it against your body!

1 + 1 v. 2

Goalkeeper plus Defender versus Two Attackers

The defender has to stop the attacker with the ball in such a way that a direct breakthrough or shot becomes impossible and passing to the other attacker is difficult. The primary objective is to slow down the attack and improve the defense's position.

Meanwhile, you should move in so that the attacker can't shoot directly or chip the ball over your head. At the same time, you should be trying to get into a good position in case the attacker with the ball manages to pass to a teammate.

If the attacker does pass, you have a choice to make: Should you rush out of the goal to stop the receiver, or is your teammate in a better position to stop the receiver with a quick move to the side? Communicate your decision to your teammate with a few quick words.

If you leave the goal to stop the attacker, the defender should move in front of the goal, ready either to block a shot or to attack the other attacker in case the ball gets passed back.

If the second attacker does pass back, now the defender has to decide whether to rush out of the goal and stop the receiver, or to let the goalkeeper do it.

- In every case, the defender tells the goalkeeper what's going on.
- **Important**: The rear player always makes the decision and directs the player in front.

Sample Exercise

EXERCISE

Attacker A and Defender C play inside a 15-yard-square field just outside the penalty box. The second attacker (B) has a ball and stands outside this field.

A starts the exercise with a quick opening run toward B. As soon as B passes to A, B moves onto the field, starting a 2 v. 1 on a goal with goalkeeper.

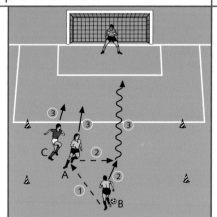

FOCUS ON

- getting into a position that allows you to get involved easily
- cooperating with your defender (communication!)

VARIATIONS

1. A one-touches the ball back to B before starting the attack on the goal.
2. As soon as A starts the showing run, B can move onto the field and decide whether to pass to A or not.
3. A and B both start out outside the field.
4. C and the goalkeeper can counterattack on a goal line.
5. After winning the ball, C and the goalkeeper can score a point by passing, shooting or throwing the ball through a five-yard-wide goal directly opposite their goal, 36 yards away.

1 v. 1 in the Air

Goalkeeper's Tactics

This situation can arise anytime you leave the goal on a high cross or frontal shot. You then have two options:

You can try to intercept the ball, or, if there are too many players near the goal and there's a high risk of losing the ball after you catch it, you can knock it out of the danger zone.

Regardless of which option you choose, the situation can develop in one of three ways:

a) The ball is moving directly toward a stationary opponent.

This is the easiest situation, since it allows you to get a running start and then jump for the ball.

b) The ball is going between you and an opponent who is running toward the goal.

This is a difficult situation, since both players are moving toward the ball and therefore toward each other. You should take off with the leg that's farther away from your opponent and bring your other knee up somewhat to keep your opponent away from you (protect yourself to the extent that the rules permit).

c) You're standing still, and the ball is going to go over your head.

This is a very difficult situation because your opponent gets a running start before jumping for the ball. In this case, we recommend taking several quick steps backwards so that you can get a running start too before you jump.

Always remember: Catching comes before punching – in other words, your first choice should always be to safely intercept a high ball. Punching is always your last resort! You shouldn't start practicing deflecting techniques until you've mastered all the catching techniques.

In later chapters you'll find various age-appropriate exercises for teaching goalkeepers how to deal with 1 v. 1s in the air. They all share the following objectives:

1. Safely intercepting high balls from the front or side (with and without opponents).
2. Getting used to physical contact while in the air.
3. Winning 1 v. 1s in the air.
4. Moving the game along quickly after winning a 1 v. 1 in the air.

Dealing with Back Passes

How to Practice

Thanks to the back-pass rule, the goalkeeper is frequently required to clear back passes in tight situations, and to bring poorly aimed back passes under control and pass them on despite time and opposition pressure. And yet, in spite of this, goalkeepers still spend far too little time practicing their passing and receiving techniques.

Obviously, goalkeepers don't have to become perfect field players, but a goalkeeper who can maintain control of the ball and pass well is a huge asset to any team. Take the Netherlands, for example: Their goalkeepers play an active and important role in attack-building as "extra field players," beginning at the youth level.

The extent of a youth goalkeeper's general technique training must be factored into the equation as well. By age 8 at the latest, goalkeepers should start getting experience as field players in practice (8- to 10-year-olds) and match play (10- to 12-year-olds).

What Skills Do Goalkeepers Need?

Goalkeepers need good ball technique in order to be able to play the ball as desired. They should master receiving and controlling the ball, at the very least. They should also be able to pass accurately on the ground and in the air with the insides and insteps of both feet.

- Being able to use both feet is a plus for goalkeepers too.
- Goalkeepers should radiate security and self-confidence; good technique can only help.

What can teammates do to put their goalkeeper in a good position on back passes? They can avoid dangerous situations by following these simple guidelines:

1. Pass on the ground as soon as possible, while there's still plenty of room between goalkeeper and opponents.
2. Pass to your goalkeeper's "strong" foot.
3. Try to pass from the side, so the goalkeeper can pass the ball immediately, if necessary, without having to reposition it.
4. Take your goalkeeper's technical abilities into account; make sure the speed and angle of your pass are not too hard to handle.
5. After the pass, get open again immediately so your goalkeeper has another potential receiver.
6. If things go wrong, give your goalkeeper a word of encouragement.

Meanwhile, goalkeepers should keep the following points in mind:

1. Tell your teammates what to do; either call for back passes or refuse them, depending on the situation.
2. Anticipate situations: Call for the back pass at the right moment and look for potential receivers.

3. Show self-confidence!

4. Devote your full attention to the ball, but watch teammates and opponents too.

5. Avoid risks; always choose the simplest and safest solution.

6. Make the right decision for the situation, even under pressure.

7. Show for passes *to the side of the goal*.

8. Receive the ball safely and as soon as possible.

9. On poorly aimed back passes, always move sideways first (get your body behind the ball for extra protection), then forward.

10. Decide quickly what the next move will be.

11. Pass accurately to your teammates, on the ground if possible.

12. Avoid square passes in front of an open goal.

The first touch is the most important: Kick the ball forward on the very first touch so you can execute your next move with speed and confidence.

Practicing the Back Pass

The games and exercises in the *Warm-up Programs* for each age level are ideal for practicing the technical skills required by the back pass rule (receiving, passing accurately with the insides and insteps of both feet).

The exercises below can be used at any age level, as long as you adjust their intensity and difficulty to fit the level in question.

Developing Agility and Using Both Feet

EXERCISE 1

Two goalkeepers practice with a coach (C). GK1 stands at a cone, with two more cones ahead to the right and left, each about two yards away. C and GK2 stand to the right and left as well, about eight yards away from GK1; each has a ball. GK1 moves up to the right cone, receives a pass on the ground from C and passes directly back with the right foot. Then GK1 runs quickly backwards to the middle cone and forward to the left cone, receives a pass from GK2 and passes directly back with the left foot.

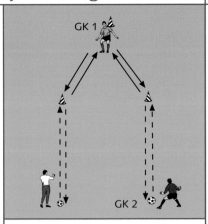

FOCUS ON
• using both feet
• developing agility

VARIATION

Only C has a ball. GK1 receives it and passes diagonally with the right foot to GK2, then runs quickly backwards to the middle cone. Then GK1 runs to the left cone, receives the ball from GK2 and kicks a direct diagonal pass to C.

EXERCISE 2

Two goalkeepers practice with a coach (C). GK1 stands at a cone, with two more cones ahead to the right and left, each about two yards away. C and GK2 stand to the right and left as well, about eight yards away from GK1; only C has a ball.
C kicks the ball so that GK1 can intercept it on the way to the left cone and pass it directly with the left foot to GK2. Then GK1 runs backwards to the middle cone and forward to the right cone, receives the ball from GK2 and passes directly with the right foot to C.

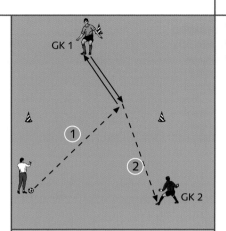

FOCUS ON
• see Exercise 1

VARIATION

GK1 runs around the middle cone.

EXERCISE 3

Setup is the same as above. The coach (C) passes on the ground to GK1, who passes directly back with the right foot, runs backwards to the middle cone and then immediately runs back to the right cone. Now C passes to GK1's right foot, and GK1 passes diagonally to GK2 before running back to the middle cone. Now the exercise starts over from the beginning, but on the other side of the field.

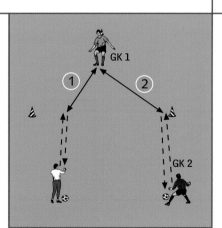

FOCUS ON
• see Exercise 1

VARIATION

GK1 passes diagonally on the second touch, not the first.

Exercises without a Goal

EXERCISE 1

Four goalkeepers practice together. Using cones, mark out a 5 x 10-yard rectangle. One goalkeeper stands at each cone. GK1 has a ball and passes it with the inside of the right foot to GK2, who repositions it with the left foot and then passes diagonally with the right to GK3, who repositions it with the right foot and passes with the left to GK4. GK4 repositions the ball with the right foot and passes diagonally with the left foot to GK1, who takes the ball diagonally forward with the left foot and passes with the right foot to GK2, and so on.

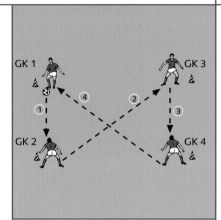

NOTE
- Goalkeepers should switch roles and positions after several rounds (you can change the direction of play as well).

VARIATIONS

1. Use two balls; GK1 and GK3 start the exercise simultaneously.
2. GK1 and GK4 form a pair, as do GK2 and GK3. GK1 and GK2 each have a ball. They kick carefully aimed diagonal passes with the inside of the foot on the ground to their partners. Receivers receive on the first touch, take the ball diagonally forward and pass diagonally back to their partners. Each player must pass accurately to avoid hitting the other pair's ball. The coach indicates which foot to use for receiving and which for passing.

EXERCISE 2

Using four cones, mark out three goals side by side (three, two and three yards wide) in front of the goalkeeper. The coach (C) has a ball and stands about five yards behind the goals. If C passes the ball through the middle goal, the goalkeeper takes it sideways on the first touch and kicks it back to C through one of the side goals on the second. If C passes through the left goal, the goalkeeper passes back directly with the left foot (same on the right).

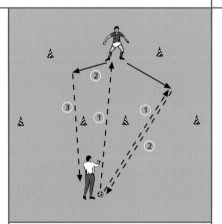

FOCUS ON
- using both feet
- receiving and controlling the ball

VARIATION

C throws the ball; the goalkeeper has to head it back through the middle goal and volley it back through the side goals.

EXERCISE 3

Goalkeepers 1 and 2 stand 10 yards apart inside two marked 3 x 3-yard fields, facing one another. GK1 passes on the ground to GK2, who receives and takes the ball to the right with the left foot, then passes back outside the fields with the right foot. GK2 moves back to the middle while GK1 runs to the left, kicks the ball back into the middle with the left foot and then passes with the right back to GK2. GK2 receives with the right foot and takes the ball to the left, then passes back outside the fields with the left. GK1 runs to the right, kicks the ball back into the middle with the right foot and passes with the left back to GK2, etc.

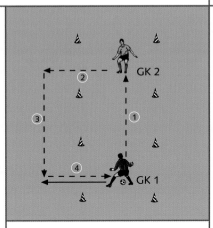

FOCUS ON

• using both feet
• switching roles after several rounds

VARIATIONS

1. Goalkeepers always use the same foot to kick and pass.
2. Goalkeepers use the inside of the foot or the instep to pass.
3. Goalkeepers keep the ball in the air while inside the field, then volley to their partner after several touches. They can receive outside the field but must be inside to pass.

EXERCISE 4

Three goalkeepers practice together. GK1 stands at a cone; GK2 and GK3 stand at two more cones to the right and left, about 10 yards away. GK1 shows for a pass from the side, and GK2 passes on the ground. With the right foot, GK1 takes the ball forward and left, then passes with the left to GK3. Then GK1 moves back to the starting cone, shows for a pass from the left, receives the pass on the ground, repositions the ball with the left foot and passes with the right, and so on.

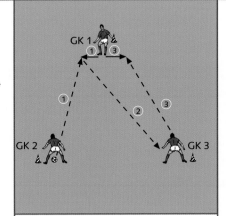

NOTE

• This simulates shifting play to the opposite side of the field. Two touches (one to receive and one to pass) should be enough!

VARIATIONS

1. GK1 passes directly, alternating feet.
2. Increase the distances; all players can pass on the ground or in the air.

EXERCISE 5

Three goalkeepers practice together, one at each corner of a triangle measuring 25 yards on each side. They pass back and forth on the ground with the instep; each player has to receive with one foot and then pass with the other. Ideally, they should take the ball diagonally forward on the first touch, then pass directly – in other words, play with only two touches.

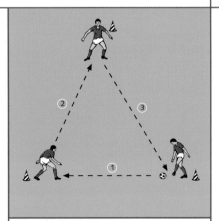

VARIATIONS

1. As soon as a player receives the ball, the coach calls out the type of pass ("ground" or "high"). The goalkeeper must react quickly.
2. Players kick low passes in the air. Important: When receiving a poorly aimed pass, move sideways first, then forward.
3. Use two (or three) balls at the same time.

NOTE

• Reverse the direction of play after several rounds; goalkeepers practice receiving, repositioning and passing the ball with the weak foot as well as the strong.

EXERCISE 6

Set up two 7-yard-wide goals 30 yards apart. GK1 and GK3 stand in the goals, GK2 in the middle.
GK1 passes on the ground to GK2, who passes directly back, a bit to one side of GK1, then turns to face GK3. With the right instep, GK1 passes directly on the ground to GK3's left foot. GK3 passes directly (if possible) to GK2, who passes directly back, a bit to one side again, then turns to face GK1. With the right instep, GK3 passes directly on the ground to GK1's left foot, etc.

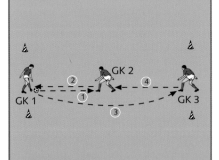

VARIATIONS

GK1 and GK3 pass to each other in the air, but they still pass on the ground to GK2.

NOTE

• After several rounds, players should switch positions and the direction of play, passing with the left foot instead.

EXERCISE 7

Four goalkeepers practice together in a field half. Set up four 7-yard-wide goals, each one five yards away from one edge of the half: A and C parallel to the centerline and endline, B and D parallel to the sidelines. Play moves counterclockwise: GK1 takes the ball diagonally forward with the left foot, then passes with the right instep on the ground to GK2, who repositions the ball with the left and passes with the right to GK3, who shows in front of Goal A for the pass from the left, etc.

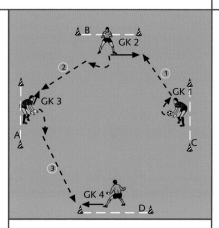

VARIATIONS

1. Use two balls at the same time; GK1 and GK3 start out with one apiece.
2. Change the type of pass to low or high passes in the air.
3. Take away one goal: Players follow their passes to the next goal.
4. Add more goalkeepers: Players follow their passes to the next goal.

NOTE

• Reverse the direction of play after several rounds.

EXERCISE 8

Setup is the same as Exercise 7. GK1 and GK3 form a pair, as do GK2 and GK4.
One player in each pair has a ball and starts play with a hard instep kick on the ground.

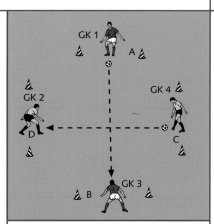

VARIATION

Use four balls at once. Two of the goalkeepers pass on the ground, the other two in the air. This variation is a serious technical challenge for goalkeepers.

NOTES

• Players should alternate feet when receiving passes, always passing with the other foot.
• Both pairs practice simultaneously; players should avoid ball collisions.

Exercises with a Goal

EXERCISE 1

Two goalkeepers practice together. GK1 stands three yards in front of the goal. GK2 stands five yards farther out, on a 10-yard-long line marked with cones. The coach (C) has a ball and stands 20 yards in front of the goal. C passes on the ground to GK1. Meanwhile, GK2 moves along the line to block GK1's view, letting the ball go past on one side or between his legs. GK1 receives and controls the ball and passes back to C.

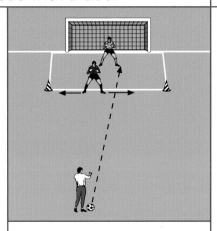

NOTE

- Players should switch roles and positions after several rounds.

VARIATIONS

1. Instead of passing back to C, GK1 plays a wall pass with GK2 first, then passes directly back to C.
2. Like Variation 1, except GK1 passes in the air (low or high).
3. Place another cone opposite the center of the goal, three yards in front of GK2. As soon as C kicks the ball toward the goal, GK2 runs around this cone and attacks GK1.

EXERCISE 2

In front of a goal, mark out four 7 x 9-yard fields, forming a large rectangle. The goalkeeper takes the position shown at right. The coach (C) has a ball and stands 25 yards in front of the goal. C passes, either on the ground into one of the front fields or in the air into one of the rear ones. On passes on the ground, the goalkeeper passes back to C directly; high passes must be controlled first, then passed back on the ground or in the air. The goalkeeper returns to the starting position after each play.

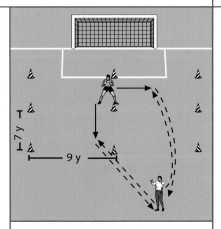

FOCUS ON

- developing general technical skills
- receiving high passes safely

VARIATIONS

1. A second goalkeeper functions as semi-active opponent.
2. A second goalkeeper stands in the front right field; C passes into the rear left field. GK2 runs into that field and attacks GK1.

EXERCISE 3

Three goalkeepers practice together. GK1 stands in the middle of a standard goal; GK2 and GK3 stand on the goal box line opposite the two goal posts and act as passers (each has a ball). The coach (C) stands on the goal box line between them.
GK1 moves to the right, receives a pass on the ground from GK2, passes back directly with the right foot and immediately dives to the left to stop a shot on the ground from C. GK1 rolls the ball back to C and returns to the center of the goal, and the exercise begins again, but on the other side this time.

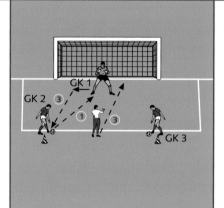

After three rounds on each side, take a short break, then switch goalkeepers.

NOTES
- If you only have one goalkeeper, field players can act as passers.
- All three goalkeepers should pass as precisely as possible.

EXERCISE 4

Three goalkeepers practice together with a coach (C). GK1 stands on the inside left, on the penalty box line; GK2 has a ball and stands five yards beyond GK1. Cones mark a 2-yard-wide goal at the penalty spot, and GK3 stands directly behind it. C has a ball and stands on the inside right, seven yards away from the big goal. GK2 passes on the ground to GK1's left foot. GK1 takes the ball forward and to the right, passes through the small goal to GK3 on the second touch and immediately dives for a shot on the ground from C, on the right side.
Repeat six times, then have goalkeepers switch roles and

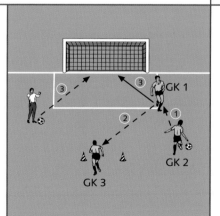

positions. Once each goalkeeper has played every position, start over again on the other side of the field. Don't forget breaks!

FOCUS ON
- developing general technical skills
- goalkeeper-specific condition training

EXERCISE 5

Two goalkeepers practice together with a coach (C). GK1 stands in a standard goal at the end of a row of three cones. C stands ten yards in front of the goal, and GK2 stands on the side, five yards away from the cones; each has a ball. C passes on the ground to GK1's left foot; GK1 switches the ball to the right and dribbles down the row of cones with that foot, then passes on the ground to C. GK2 throws the ball in a high arc toward the goal. GK1 runs after it and deflects it over the goal. On the next round, C drop-kicks to GK1.

NOTES

- GK1 should use both feet to receive and dribble, alternating from round to round.
- Goalkeepers should switch positions after several rounds.

EXERCISE 6

One goalkeeper practices with the coach (C). The goalkeeper stands on the goal line in a standard goal, with one arm extended and a hand on the left post. C has several balls and stands about six yards in front of the center of the goal. C kicks the first ball on the ground toward the right post. The goalkeeper runs over and knocks it to the side with a slide tackle, gets up quickly and dives back to the left for another shot on the ground from C.

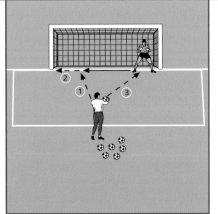

NOTE

- The goalkeeper should try to knock the first ball across the sideline, not the endline (you can station another goalkeeper on the sideline as a marker).

VARIATIONS

1. The goalkeeper starts out lying face down (head toward the right post), executes the slide tackle as above and then dives for a low shot in the air.
2. The goalkeeper clears one ball to the right, then another to the left before diving to the side for a shot on the ground.
3. The goalkeeper clears six balls in rapid succession, aiming them at small goals marked by cones and placed in various positions: three balls with the right foot and three with the left (goalkeeper-specific endurance training).

EXERCISE 7

One goalkeeper practices with the coach (C). The goalkeeper stands about eight yards in front of the goal, facing away from it. C has several balls and stands at the penalty spot. C kicks the first ball past the goalkeeper on the right, toward the goal. The goalkeeper immediately clears it to the right with a slide tackle, then gets up quickly and dives for a low shot in the air on the other side. C kicks the next ball past the goalkeeper on the left, etc.

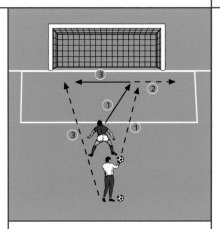

VARIATION

C shoots to the left and right in no predictable pattern.

EXERCISE 8

The goalkeeper stands at the penalty spot opposite the center of the goal. Two more goals are placed or marked to the left and right, each about 30 yards away. Another goalkeeper stands in each of these goals to retrieve balls. The coach stands 15 yards in front of the goalkeeper with several balls and shoots them in various ways. The goalkeeper tries to catch them as quickly as possible and pass them to the two small goals.

VARIATIONS

1. The goalkeeper must shoot directly at the small goals.
2. An opponent (second goalkeeper) puts pressure on the goalkeeper.

EXERCISE 9

Three goalkeepers practice together. GK1 stands in a standard goal; GK2 stands 20 yards in front of the goal, behind a eight-yard-wide goal marked by cones. GK3 has a number of balls and stands 15 yards behind the goal. GK3 kicks the ball over the goal to GK2, who receives it in front of the small goal, then shoots with a well-aimed instep kick. If GK2 scores, players switch positions.

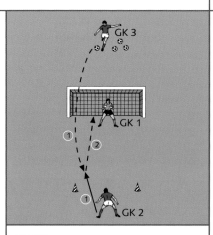

NOTE
• A field player can play GK2's position.

VARIATION

GK3 throws, punts or drop-kicks the ball over the goal, and GK2 plays 1 v. 1 against GK1 to score.

EXERCISE 10

GK1 stands in the center of the goal box line; the coach (C) has several balls and stands three yards farther out. GK2 has a ball and stands 18 yards in front of the goal. C kicks shots on the ground past GK1 on the right and left; GK1 moves from side to side to pass each ball back directly, using whichever foot is closer to the ball. Occasionally, C kicks a shot so far to the side that GK1 has to dive to block it. At that moment, GK2 runs up to take a well-aimed instep shot. GK1 gets up quickly and tries to get to this shot as well. If GK2 scores, the goalkeepers switch roles.

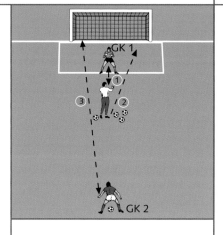

VARIATION

Instead of shooting on the ground past GK1, C throws low balls in the air. GK1 volleys these back to C. Suddenly, C throws the ball high up in the air. GK1 catches it (C can function as a semi-active or fully active opponent here) and immediately rolls it to GK2. As soon as GK1 catches the ball, GK2 runs up and tries to score on an instep kick.

EXERCISE 11

GK1 stands near the penalty spot; the coach (C) has several balls and stands five yards beyond GK1, on the left. GK2 stands on the right, 15 yards beyond GK1. C kicks a hard pass on the ground to GK1, who takes the ball to the right (using the left foot) and then passes with the right foot to GK2. Now C kicks a shot on the ground at the near post; GK1 executes a roll, then moves to deflect this shot to the left. Finally, GK2 tries to get a well-aimed half-volley past GK1.

NOTE
- Goalkeepers switch positions after several rounds and eventually start over again on the other side of the field.

EXERCISE 12

GK1 stands in the center of a standard goal. Using cones, mark out three small goals (A, B, and C) 10 yards away. The coach (C) has a ball and stands 10 yards beyond Goal A. GK2 stands behind Goals B and C. C passes on the ground through Goal A. GK1 receives it and passes through the goal indicated by GK2. Then GK2 passes on the ground back through the same goal to GK1, who passes through the goal indicated by C.

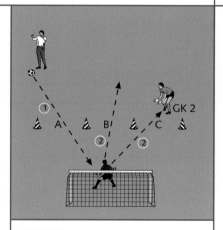

NOTES
- GK1 should make eye contact with GK2 just as C passes.
- Goalkeepers switch roles after several rounds.

VARIATIONS
1. GK1 passes with one touch every time.
2. C and GK2 pass in the air (low or high), and GK1 passes back on the ground.
3. All three pass in the air (low or high).

Back Pass Games

GAME 1

Each team designates a starting goalkeeper, who is replaced only if the opposition scores.

All players are allowed to use their hands at any time to defend or win the ball; however, they must use their feet to pass. If the ball crosses the sideline, the attackers have to dribble it back onto the field before shooting. If it crosses the endline, the goalkeeper puts it back into play, and attackers must complete one pass before shooting. The back pass rule applies to everyone. Slide tackling to block shots is not allowed. Which team can score more goals?

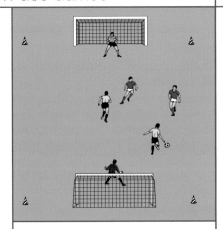

SETUP
- 3 v. 3 on two five-yard-wide goals in a 15 x 15-yard field

GAME 2

Four players pass back and forth and try to keep their two opponents from winning the ball. A player who does win the ball can shoot immediately. If the shot is successful, that player trades positions with the player who failed to block the shot; if not, with the player whose pass was intercepted. The back pass rule applies to the goalkeeper.

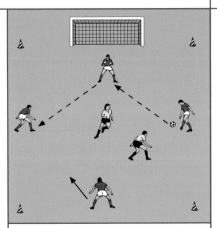

SETUP
- 4 v. 2 on a 5-yard-wide goal in a 10 x 15-yard field
- One player from the team of four stands in the goal, and one stands on each sideline.

GAME 3

Four goalkeepers (or three goalkeepers plus a coach or field player) pass back and forth. The goalkeeper in the middle tries to touch the ball (= one point) or even win it (= two points). No player should spend more than 45 to 60 seconds in the middle. Which goalkeeper can score the most points?

SETUP
• 4 v. 1 in a 5 x 5-yard field

GAME 4

Two teams of two (plus their goalkeepers) play in a field. Goalkeepers are allowed to shoot from inside their own half; field players are not.

SETUP
• 2 (+ goalkeeper) v. 2 (+ goalkeeper) on two standard goals in a 20 x 30-yard field with a centerline (marked by cones)

GAME 5

The larger team kicks a well-aimed shot on the ground or in the air and immediately puts pressure on the goalkeeper. If the defenders win the ball, the goalkeeper joins the counter-attack.

SETUP

- 3 v. 2 (or 4 v. 3) on a standard goal with goalkeeper and two "countergoals"
- The back pass rule applies to the goalkeeper.

GAME 6

The goalkeeper of the smaller team is allowed to touch the ball with his hands; the other goalkeeper is not. The goal-keeper of the larger team kicks a well-aimed pass in the air to a teammate on the sideline, and the team begins its attack. If their opponents win the ball, they can coun-terattack. Both goalkeepers are allowed to shoot like field players and participate in at-tack building.

SETUP

- 4 v. 6 on two standard goals with goal-keepers
- Field size depends on age and ability level.

VARIATION

Both goalkeepers are allowed to use their hands. The small-er team can also try to score on two small goals five yards to the left and right of the opposition's main goal.

GAME 7

Only the smaller team has a goalkeeper, who can try to score on the two small goals with an instep kick after a back pass or with a throw or drop-kick after catching a cross or shot.

The goalkeeper functions as a designated receiver for the rest of the team.

Six-second rule: The goalkeeper may use this time as desired, depending on the situation.

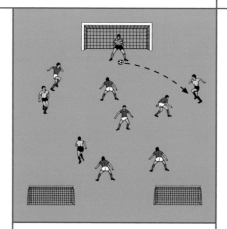

SETUP

- 4 v. 6 on a standard goal with goalkeeper and two small "countergoals"
- Field size depends on age and ability level.

GAME 8

There are no restrictions on this game, except that one player from the defending team must always leave the field (advantage to the attackers). Goalkeepers should be actively involved in the game and are allowed to score.

SETUP

- 6 v. 6 with two goalkeepers on two standard goals (field size: double the penalty box)

Basic Ball Training

Trying It on for Size: Ages 8 to 10

In principle, players at this age level should not be specializing yet, and that includes the goalkeeper's position. Age-appropriate practice sessions should focus on comprehensive, versatile technique and coordination training, using playful methods to teach soccer-specific techniques such as ball handling and short-range passing. Fortunately, there are plenty of 8- to 10-year-olds who take pride and pleasure in standing in the goal. As a coach, you should take advantage of this fact to teach goalkeeping to as many players as possible; you're sure to discover some future goalkeepers in the process. The exercises presented in this chapter make up a "basic ball training" program designed to prepare players for all aspects of the game, including goalkeeping.

A player's introduction to goalkeeping should be easy and fun.

Guidelines for Working with 8- to 10-Year-Olds

Becoming a Well-Rounded Player

8- to 10-year-olds stand on the threshold of the so-called "golden age of learning." It's the perfect time to teach them the basics of the game's essential techniques.

Important: Players can forget movements/techniques just as quickly as they learn them!

• Coordination, both of individual muscles and of muscle groups, responds well to training at this age level.

• Concentrate on focused coordination training, combined with technique training; finely coordinated movements are rarely successful.

• This is a "critical phase" for training agility and reaction speed.

• "Playful" calisthenics lay the foundation for good mobility in the future.

• Abstract thinking and the capacity for planning and tactical play are not well-developed yet.

• Avoid pure position-specific training.

• Players should learn the basics of all soccer-specific technical skills through exercises with the ball, and then apply them in practice games.

• Physical intensity should be kept at a relatively low but continuous level.

• Even at this age level, players have to be able to concentrate, but don't expect them to do it for more than short periods. As soon as you notice that your players are losing their focus, you need to reawaken their excitement with motivational exercises and games. After the fun, you can go back to another focused practice period.

• The children themselves can help determine how long their breaks should be.

• Good organization can prevent long periods of "down time."

• Concentrate on clearing up the major problems; you can do this easily with focused discussions and simple corrections.

• You have to demonstrate technical sequences and basic tactics, so that your players can begin to comprehend the movements involved.

• You'll have to be satisfied with "small" improvements.

• In soccer training, exercises that are interesting, highly active and versatile create motivation.

• End every practice session with a motivational exercise (competition).

The Bottom Line: Every training program should move from easy to hard, and from simple to complex.

Becoming a Goalkeeper

Coordination Training and Dexterity Exercises

At this age level, the desire to play is very strong. Eight- to 10-year-olds seem to be highly motivated in most situations, and often they can't wait for practice. They tend to have good attitudes, a strong urge to be active, loads of energy and a love of adventure. Their curiosity about anything new and unknown is the main force motivating them in practice and match play.

As a coach, your first job is actually to reduce the level of excitement so that you can start training. There are plenty of exercises that are good for this; for example:

Goalkeeper Tennis:

Four players play in a 5 x 4-yard field. You'll need a "magic rope," four cones, and the most level ground you can find.

Two players stand on each side of the rope, throwing and catching the ball. Field size depends on ability level. By taking just a few quick steps, players should be able to reach each ball before it hits the ground.

The following rules apply: The ball is not allowed to touch the ground! If it does, or if it goes out of the field, it goes to the opposition. To increase motivation, play up to a certain score; the losers have to do an extra exercise.

Goalkeeper Tennis

EXERCISE 1

2 v. 2 with several restrictions:
1. Players start by throwing the ball from over their heads (throw-in style).
2. Afterwards, they volley back and forth.
3. After throwing or volleying, each player sits down and quickly stands up again. This speeds up the game.

VARIATIONS

1. After throwing or volleying, each player lies face-down or executes a forward or backward roll and quickly stands up again.
2. Use different balls (mini soccer balls, tennis balls, etc.).

OBJECTIVES

- motivational warm-up
- coordination training
- technique training

EXERCISE 2

2 x 1 v. 1 with several restrictions:

One player from Team A and one from Team B stand on each side of the rope. The player who has the ball throws it over the rope, and A and B both try to gain control of the ball, using their hands. Players score one point for their team each time they win the ball and then complete a pass to the other side.

1 v. 1 play only occurs while players are receiving the ball; they're not allowed to interfere while their opponents are throwing.

OBJECTIVES

- motivational warm-up
- coordination training
- technique training
- learning to be assertive and fight for the ball
- learning to cooperate

VARIATIONS

1. Players have to volley back and forth (you may need to enlarge the field).
2. Use different balls (mini soccer balls, tennis balls, etc.).

EXERCISE 3

3 v. 3:

Each side of the field is divided into three fields (see illustration). Each player is responsible for one field and must stay inside it.

Also:

Players in the fields closest to the rope are only allowed to throw the ball; players in the rear fields must volley.

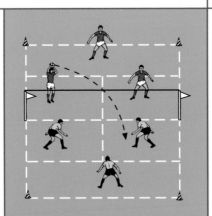

OBJECTIVES

- motivational warm-up
- coordination training
- technique training

VARIATIONS

1. After throwing or volleying, each player sits down, lies face-down or executes a forward or backward roll, and quickly stands up again.
2. Use different balls (mini soccer balls, tennis balls, etc.).

Touch Games

EXERCISE 1

3 v. 3 (4 v. 4) in a marked field:
Two teams play in a 7 x 10-yard field, throwing and catching a single ball. Teams score one point each time they complete a certain number of touches without letting their opponents touch the ball. The first team to reach three points wins. Losers do an extra exercise. If the ball touches the ground or goes out of the field, it goes to the opposition. Players can only win the ball in the air; touching the player who has the ball is not allowed, but crowding is.

OBJECTIVES
• motivational warm-up
• coordination training
• technique training
• learning to be assertive and fight for the ball
• learning to cooperate

VARIATIONS
1. Players have to crawl on the ground.
2. Use different balls.
3. Players are not allowed to cross a marked zone in the middle of the field.
4. If the number of players is uneven, one becomes a "neutral" passer who helps whichever team has the ball.

EXERCISE 2

3 v. 3 in marked fields:
Three pairs play 1 v. 1 in three fields. Players must stay inside their own fields while throwing or volleying.

Rules are as above.
The fields can be arranged in various ways:
– three adjacent fields of the same size,
– three fields of the same size "randomly" distributed (e.g. two fields side by side and one in front of them).

OBJECTIVE
• See Exercise 1

VARIATIONS
1. Players switch fields (moving clockwise) after a certain period of time.
2. Players must move a certain way: running, crawling, rolling.

Touch Games with Small Goals

EXERCISE 1

2 v. 2 (3 v. 3) in a marked field:
Two teams of two (or three) play in a 10 x 7-yard field with a small goal in the middle of each of its long sides. Players can only move by crawling. The player who has the ball cannot move and can be crowded, but not touched. If the ball goes out of the field, it goes to the opposition. Any player can score a goal, from any distance. Players are only allowed to throw the ball.

OBJECTIVE

● See Exercise 1 under "Touch Games"

VARIATIONS

- Players throw the ball.
- Players roll the ball.
- Players can move the ball any way they want.
- Players must reach a designated marker before shooting.
- Use different balls (mini soccer balls, tennis balls, etc.).

If the number of players is uneven, one becomes a "neutral" passer who helps whichever team has the ball.

EXERCISE 2

2 v. 2 (3 v. 3) in a marked field:
Players use their feet to pass, and try to score on small goals.

Setup is as above.

OBJECTIVE

● See Exercise 1 under "Touch Games"

VARIATIONS

1. Players must reach a designated marker before shooting.
2. Players are allowed to use their hands to defend inside marked goal boxes.
3. Players can use their hands anytime to win the ball, but afterwards they have to pass with their feet again.
4. Use different balls (mini soccer balls, tennis balls, etc.).

Throwing Exercises

Throwing and catching in a group:
A number of players sit in a circle on the ground. First they throw one ball back and forth at random. After a short time, a second ball is added. Throwing both balls to the same player is not allowed. Any player who drops a ball, aims poorly or throws to a player who is already holding one ball receives a negative point. Players must leave the circle when they reach a given number of negative points. Play continues until only two players are left.

OBJECTIVES
- motivational warm-up
- coordination training
- increasing motivation

Dexterity Exercises

EXERCISE 1
Dexterity and ball technique:
Several players move about in a 6-yard-square field; each one has a ball.
1. While walking or running, players dribble the ball with the right hand only (switching to the other hand after a designated period of time).
2. While walking or jogging, they dribble by hand, alternating between left and right.
3. While walking or jogging, they dribble with their hands. After a few steps, they give the ball a high bounce, spin around quickly and continue dribbling.

OBJECTIVES
- motivational warm-up
- coordination training
- developing a feel for the ball
- increasing motivation

VARIATIONS
Like 2, above, except players roll the ball instead of dribbling it.
Like 3, except instead of spinning, players sit down (or lie face-down) and quickly stand up again.
Like 3, except players execute a forward or backward roll.
Like 3, except players run under the ball, turn 180° and continue dribbling in the opposite direction.

EXERCISE 2

Dexterity and ball technique: Several players and a coach (C) move about in a 6-yard-square field. Cones mark the corners of the field, and another cone stands in the center of each sideline. Each player has a ball and dribbles it by hand, alternating between left and right. C calls out a player's name, and that player throws a high ball to C. C throws it up, and the player catches it in the air, then resumes dribbling.

VARIATIONS

1. Before catching the ball in the air, players must execute a coordination exercise (forward or backward roll, turn 360°, etc.).
2. Instead of throwing the ball up, C gives it a high bounce off the ground in front of the player.
3. Players must execute a forward roll toward a cone, run around it and then catch the ball.
4. Players must crawl between C's legs before catching the ball.

OBJECTIVES
- motivational warm-up
- coordination training
- technique training
- developing a feel for the ball
- increasing motivation
- learning new techniques

EXERCISE 3

Dexterity and ball technique: Setup is as above.

Players dribble their balls with their feet, without losing them or colliding. The coach (C) calls out a player's name, and that player passes accurately to C, executes a backward roll and dives sideways to save a shot on the ground from C, then resumes dribbling.

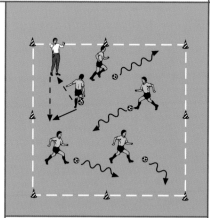

VARIATIONS

1. The player must execute a forward roll toward a cone, run around it and then dive sideways to stop C's shot on the ground.
2. The player passes to C and then stands with legs apart. C passes back between the player's legs, and the player dives backwards for the ball.
3. After C passes between the player's legs, the player executes a backward roll, quickly turns 180° and dives forward for the ball.

OBJECTIVES
- See above

Throwing Exercises for Pairs

EXERCISE 1

Partners stand five yards apart, facing one another, and throw two balls back and forth.

Player 1 throws one ball straight up in the air. Player 2 throws the other ball to Player 1, who catches it and throws it back quickly, so as to be able to catch the first ball before it hits the ground. Players switch roles after five to eight rounds.

VARIATION

Use different balls, or have players throw and catch while sitting on the ground.

OBJECTIVES

- increasing motivation
- coordination training
- developing a feel for the ball
- learning running and movement techniques

EXERCISE 2

Partners stand five yards apart, facing one another, and throw one ball back and forth:

1. Players throw with one hand and catch with two.
2. Players throw and catch with one hand.
3. Players follow a certain pattern, for example: Player 1 throws with the right hand to Player 2's left hand. 2 throws diagonally to 1's left hand, who throws back with the left hand to 2's right. 2 throws diagonally to 1's right hand, and so on. Players switch roles after four or five rounds.

VARIATIONS

1. Players bounce the ball off the ground in front of each other.
2. Player 1 has the ball and calls out the command to start, then gives the ball a high bounce. At Player 1's signal, Player 2 executes a coordination exercise and catches the ball (e.g. "Go!" – bounce the ball – turn 360° – catch the ball with both hands behind the back).
3. Use different balls (mini soccer balls, tennis balls, etc.).

OBJECTIVE

- See Exercise 1

EXERCISE 3

Partners stand three or four yards apart, facing one another, and throw one ball back and forth:

1. Combine throwing with coordination exercises: After throwing, Player 1 executes a quick 360° turn (alternating between turning to the right and to the left) or a forward or backward roll.
2. Partners trade positions: Player 1 throws the ball up in the air and moves to Player 2's position. Player 2 takes quick, short steps to Player 1's position and catches the ball with one hand.

OBJECTIVE

• See Exercise 1

VARIATIONS

1. Partners stand closer together and use both hands: Player 1 throws with both hands to Player 2, who catches it with both hands behind the back, brings it around to the front and throws to Player 1. Catching behind the back is easier if you stand under the ball and then take a small step forward just before catching it.
2. Use different balls (mini soccer balls, tennis balls, etc.).

EXERCISE 4

Partners stand three or four yards apart. Each one holds a ball.

1. At the coach's signal, both players throw to each other, one high and the other low to prevent collisions.
2. Each player holds a ball in the right hand. At the coach's signal, both throw to their partner's left hand, then with left to the right hand, etc.
3. One partner holds both balls and throws them simultaneously.

OBJECTIVES

• increasing motivation
• coordination training
• developing a feel for the ball
• staying constantly in motion and standing on the balls of the feet (staying light on your feet)

VARIATIONS

1. Players must throw diagonally (switch to the other hand after several rounds).
2. Use different balls (mini soccer balls, tennis balls, etc.).
3. Use different balls and have players throw and catch while sitting on the ground.

10- to 12-Year-Olds:
The Start of Focused Training

The goals and methods of intermediate training follow naturally from what has already been accomplished in basic training. The main focus is on the systematic teaching of goalkeeper-specific techniques and their application to game situations. Practice sessions and exercises are structured quite differently at this level than at the next; even though 12- to 14-year-olds also fall under the heading of "intermediate training."

Typical Player Characteristics

• This is the best age level for teaching as players are ready to learn, eager to get involved and not afraid to take chances.
• Players still have a strong desire to move around and play.
• They are also developing a desire to get physical with the other players, to compete and win.
• Strength, power and leverage all improve, and fine motor coordination has the potential to be excellent.
• Players are increasingly brave and willing to take risks in 1 v. 1 play. In their handling of opponents and the ball, they show more spontaneity and creativity than ever.
• The capacity for planned (tactical) action within limited parameters increases. This is an ideal situation for refining the techniques players have already learned in crude form — take advantage of it!
• The primary objective for the player learning to execute each movement precisely.

BVB Dortmund's Jens Lehmann (German 1st Division): excellent goalkeeping technique on the line and in front of it.

- In the case of mistakes, individual conversations and corrections (with the help of solo exercises) are invaluable.
- Players practice each technique alone at first, then in combination with others; technique and coordination exercises are combined.
- Improvements in coordination increase reaction speed and running speed as well.
- Improving condition is of secondary importance, but it will become critical at the next age level. However, practice sessions should be longer and more intense than they were at the 8- to 10-year-old level.
- Exercises focused on anaerobic (high-intensity) endurance and strength are not appropriate yet.
- At this stage players begin the specialization that will lead some of them to become goal-keepers.
- Tactics are integrated into team training in general, and game situations become more realistic.

THE BOTTOM LINE:

Work your way from easy to hard, from simple to complex.

Basic Goalkeeper Technique Training

This chapter includes a number of practical exercises for teaching goalkeeper-specific techniques. For each technique, there are four basic exercise types (which represent the beginnings of specialized goalkeeper training). All of these types may be altered and/or combined.

Exercise Type 1: individual technique training

Exercise Type 2: combined technique and coordination training

Exercise Type 3: multiple player technique training

Exercise Type 4: exercises on the goal

Notes:

- Coordination training should take place during warm-up and in combination with technique exercises (see Exercise Type 2).
- Exercise Type 4 lends itself to teaching certain basic tactics—positional play, 1 v. 1 play and attack building. However, the general team training program should focus on these as well.
- Limit condition training to speed and mobility exercises in the context of coordination training.
- You can harness children's considerable powers of imagination (cognition) for the training process, and increase their willingness to get involved with skillful encouragement (motivation).
- On all exercises on the goal (Exercise Type 4), we recommend placing an extra cone in the center of the goal, for better orientation and to teach positional play.

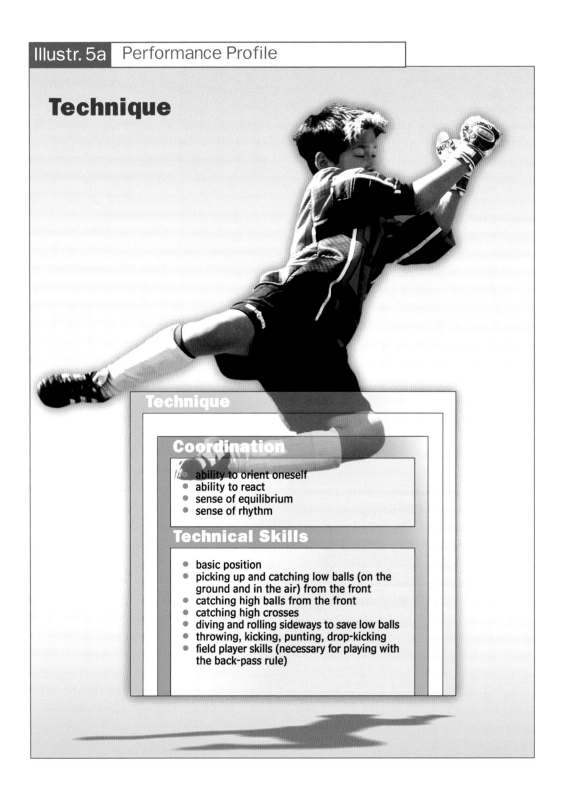

Illustr. 5a Performance Profile

Technique

Technique

Coordination

- ability to orient oneself
- ability to react
- sense of equilibrium
- sense of rhythm

Technical Skills

- basic position
- picking up and catching low balls (on the ground and in the air) from the front
- catching high balls from the front
- catching high crosses
- diving and rolling sideways to save low balls
- throwing, kicking, punting, drop-kicking
- field player skills (necessary for playing with the back-pass rule)

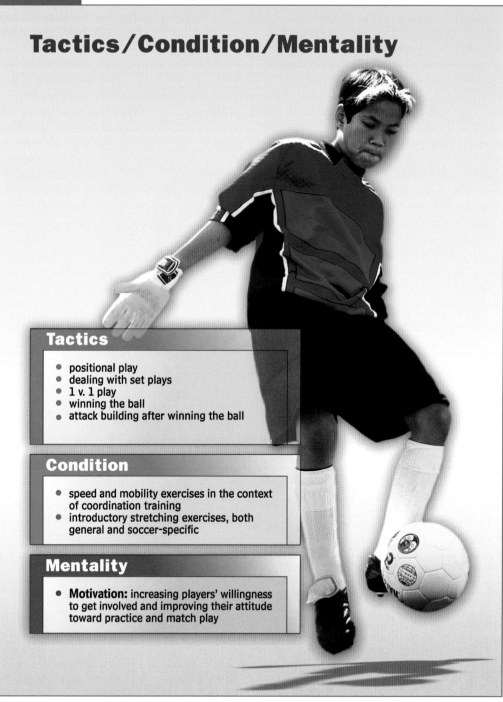

Illustr. 5b

Tactics/Condition/Mentality

Tactics

- positional play
- dealing with set plays
- 1 v. 1 play
- winning the ball
- attack building after winning the ball

Condition

- speed and mobility exercises in the context of coordination training
- introductory stretching exercises, both general and soccer-specific

Mentality

- **Motivation:** increasing players' willingness to get involved and improving their attitude toward practice and match play

Technical Skills

The Basic Position

Exercises specifically designed to teach the basic position are not included in this chapter:
• There is no single „right" basic position. The best position for the situation depends on multiple factors, such as the position of the ball, the speed of the shot and its predicted curve. The appropriate position on a cross is different from the position on a mid-range shot (see Chapter 3).
• In each of the following exercises, it is up to you, the coach, to make sure players assume the appropriate position, correcting them as necessary. Too many reminders are better than not enough, especially for young players.

Note

We also recommend combining rolling the ball with other goalkeeper-specific techniques. See exercises on the goal for catching high balls, diving and landing sideways for low balls, etc. (pp. 87–121).

Perfect technique: picking up a shot on the ground.

Individual Technique Training

BASIC EXERCISE 1

The player stands in a five-yard-wide goal. The coach (C) has a ball and stands four or five yards in front of the goal. C kicks a ground ball directly to the player, who picks it up and rolls it back to C. On each play, the player puts a different foot forward.

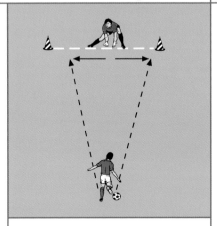

FOCUS ON
- taking a deep lunge step behind the ball, weight on the balls of the feet
- putting the right foot forward when the ball is going to the right
- putting the left foot forward when the ball is going to the left

VARIATIONS

1. C kicks the ball to the player's left or right, and the player takes a small step sideways before picking it up.
2. The player stands at a cone; C has a ball and stands four yards in front of the cone. C kicks a ground ball to the player, who picks the ball up and rolls it back to C, then runs once around the cone and assumes the basic position again. C kicks another ground ball to the player. The player puts a different foot forward on each play, and alternates running clockwise and counterclockwise around the cone.

Individual Technique and Coordination Training

BASIC EXERCISE 2

Setup is the same as Exercise 1, but now after rolling the ball back to C, the player does a forward roll, runs backwards back to the goal, assumes the basic position and awaits the next shot. On each play, the player puts a different foot forward.

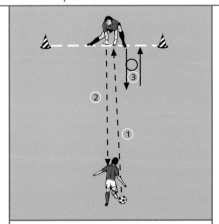

FOCUS ON
- See Exercise 1

VARIATIONS

1. The player does a backwards roll, runs forward back to the goal, assumes the basic position and awaits the next shot.
2. The player lies face-down in the middle of the goal. At a hand signal from C, the player rolls sideways in the direction indicated, assumes the basic position, picks up a ground ball from C next to the cone and rolls it back. Then the player returns to the starting position, and the exercise starts over.

Multiple Player Technique Training

BASIC EXERCISE 3

Two players stand facing each other, six yards apart. Each one stands in the middle of a five-yard-wide goal. They roll a ball back and forth, putting a different foot forward each time.

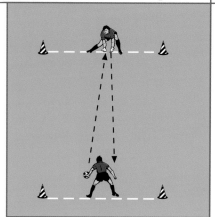

FOCUS ON
• See Exercise 1

VARIATIONS

1. Each player rolls the ball so that the other has to step sideways in order to pick it up.
2. Players roll two balls simultaneously; each rolls to the other's left. After picking up the balls, players move back to the middle of their goals and roll again. After several rounds, they start rolling to the right.

Exercises on the Goal

BASIC EXERCISE 4

GK1 stands in a five-yard-wide goal; GK2 stands eight yards away in another goal. The coach (C) has a ball and stands in the middle. C kicks a ground ball to GK2, who picks it up and rolls it at the other goal, to the left or right of GK1. GK1 tries to block the shot. If GK2 scores, the two players switch roles and positions.

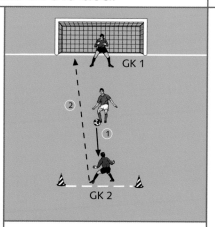

GK 1

GK 2

FOCUS ON
• See Exercise 1

VARIATION

Using cones, set up an obstacle course next to GK1's goal. GK1 stands in front of the course, away from the goal. Set up an identical course eight yards away from the goal. GK2 stands in front of this course, facing the goal. At C's command, both players run their courses, and then GK1 assumes the appropriate basic position, and GK2 tries to score by rolling the ball at the goal. If GK2 scores, the two players switch roles and positions.

Individual Technique Training

BASIC EXERCISE 1

The player stands in a five-yard-wide goal; the coach (C) has a ball and stands five yards in front of the goal. For better orientation, another cone stands behind the center of the goal (this is the player's starting point for follow-up plays). C throws a high ball to the player, who catches it, throws it back to C and returns to the basic position in front of the center cone. On each play, the player takes off with a different leg.

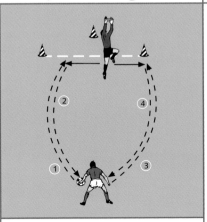

FOCUS ON
- putting your weight on the takeoff leg
- taking off with the left leg when the ball is going to the right (and vice versa)

VARIATIONS

1. C throws the ball slightly to one side of the player, who has to take a small step sideways to catch it. The player takes off with a different leg each time.
2. The player stands just to the right of the goal. C throws a high ball from the side toward the far corner of the goal. The player runs to the ball, takes off with the right leg, turns slightly toward the ball and catches it. Afterwards the player assumes the basic position at the left cone, and the exercise starts over again.

Individual Technique and Coordination Training

BASIC EXERCISE 2

Using cones, mark out a triangle (four yards on each side). The coach (C) stands four yards away from one side of it; the player stands at the opposite corner. C throws the ball toward the left and right cones alternately. The player moves (outside the triangle) as follows: high ball toward the left cone = forward toward the ball, take off with the right leg, backwards to the far cone; high ball toward the right cone = forward toward the ball, take off with the left leg, backwards to the far cone.

FOCUS ON
- putting your weight on the takeoff leg
- explosive takeoff with the takeoff leg (brief contact with the ground)

VARIATIONS

1. The player turns around once completely before moving forward and catching the ball.
2. The player does a forward roll before moving backwards.
3. The player does a backwards roll before moving backwards.

Multiple Player Technique Training

BASIC EXERCISE 3

Using cones, mark out a triangle (four yards on each side). Players line up at one side of it; each one has a ball. The coach (C) stands four yards behind the opposite corner. The first player volleys to C, runs to the far cone, touches it briefly and runs backwards to whichever cone C indicates ("one" or "two"). Then the player runs around the cone, moves to catch a high ball thrown by the coach and goes to the end of the line

VARIATION

Before moving backwards to the designated cone, the player does a backwards roll toward it. As soon as the coach yells "stop," the player stops moving backwards and runs straight to the high ball.

FOCUS ON
- putting your weight on the takeoff leg
- explosive takeoff with the takeoff leg (brief contact with the ground)

Exercises on the Goal

BASIC EXERCISE 4

GK1 stands in a five-yard-wide goal; the coach (C) has a ball and stands on the end-line, five yards to the left or right of the goal. GK2 stands at a cone 12 yards in front of the goal. C throws a high ball in front of the goal, and GK1 catches it from the side and rolls it to GK2. GK2 tries to score with a well-aimed shot (with the instep or inside of the foot). If GK2 scores, the goalkeepers switch roles and positions.

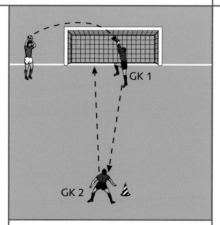

VARIATIONS

1. Instead of standing directly in front of the goal, GK2 stands at the inside left or right position.
2. C has two balls and stands at the left or right goal box corner. After GK1 catches the first ball from the side and rolls it to GK2, C shoots the second ball at the near corner of the goal. GK1 dives side-ways to save the ball, rolls it back to the coach while still on the ground and gets up quickly to stop GK2's shot.

FOCUS ON
- putting your weight on the takeoff leg
- explosive takeoff with the takeoff leg (brief contact with the ground)

Individual Technique Training

BASIC EXERCISE 1

The player has a ball and stands in the middle of a six-yard-wide goal. The player rolls the ball on the ground to the coach (C), who kicks a carefully aimed ground ball at the left side of the goal. The player takes a step to the side and dives for the ball, then gets back up. The exercise starts over again; this time C shoots at the right side.

FOCUS ON
- rolling over the hips, side and shoulder
- reaching for the ball with both hands
- securing the ball against the body

VARIATIONS
1. The player waits for C's command before going for the ball.
2. The player starts out lying face-down.

Individual Technique and Coordination Training

BASIC EXERCISE 2

Set up cones as shown in the diagram. The coach (C) has a ball and stands three yards in front of the cones. The player runs sideways between the cones and dives to the side for a ground ball from C. If the player runs to the right around the first cone, then C shoots at the right side, and vice versa (player moves left, moves right and falls sideways on the ball).

FOCUS ON
- bringing your leg forward: on a dive to the right, the left knee should come slightly forward (and vice versa) to keep you from rolling over backwards

VARIATION

The player rolls the ball back to C while still on the ground, runs backwards between the cones to the starting position and starts over again; C shoots at the other side this time.

Multiple Player Technique Training

BASIC EXERCISE 3

Two goalkeepers practice together. Each one holds a ball and stands at the right corner of a different six-yard-wide goal; the two goals are seven yards apart. At the coach's (C's) signal, each rolls a ball straight toward the opposite goal and then dives for the other's ball. Afterwards, the exercise starts over from the other corner of the goal.

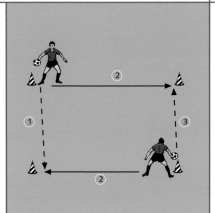

VARIATIONS

1. Instead of rolling the balls, players pass them with the inside of the foot.
2. Competition: Each goal-keeper lies face-down in the right corner of the goal, behind the ball. At C's signal, each tries to roll the ball into the other's goal while stopping the other's shot at the same time.

FOCUS ON

• rolling over the hips, side and shoulder
• "stopping the ball out in front": on a ground ball to the right, taking a short step toward it with the right foot (or vice versa) and stopping it as soon as possible

Exercises on the Goal

BASIC EXERCISE 4

GK1 stands in a five-yard-wide goal; the coach (C) has a ball and stands three yards in front of the goal. GK2 stands at a cone 12 yards in front of the goal. C passes on the ground to GK1, passing to a different foot each time; GK1 passes back directly. Suddenly C lets the ball go by, and GK2 shoots with the inside of the foot or the instep (on the ground). If GK2 scores, the goalkeepers switch roles and positions. While GK2 shoots, C remains in position to block GK1's view or deflect the shot.

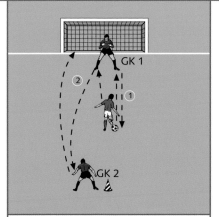

VARIATION

GK2 has a ball as well. Instead of letting the ball go by, C suddenly passes to GK1's left or right, so that GK1 has to dive sideways to stop the ball. GK1 rolls the ball back to C while still on the ground, gets up quickly and stops GK2's shot.

FOCUS ON

• reacting quickly
• rolling over the hips, side and shoulder
• reaching for the ball with both hands
• securing the ball against the body

Individual Technique Training

BASIC EXERCISE 1

The goalkeeper and the coach (C) stand facing each other, 15 yards apart, with a five-yard-wide goal between them. They punt (or volley) back and forth over the goal.

FOCUS ON

• fluid movements: after kicking the ball, swinging the leg through in the direction of the kick and taking an extra step

VARIATIONS

1. Add a second ball.
2. C moves to one side; the goalkeeper has to pass there.
3. C throws the ball over the goal to the goalkeeper, who catches it and punts (or volleys) it back.
4. C throws the ball to the goalkeeper's left or right; proceed as in Variation 3.

Individual Technique and Coordination Training

BASIC EXERCISE 2

The goalkeeper has a ball and stands in the middle of a five-yard-wide goal; the coach (C) stands 10 yards in front of the goal. First the goalkeeper punts (or volleys) or drop-kicks the ball into C's hands, then runs sideways to the left cone, touches it and catches a high ball from the side. Then the goalkeeper punts (or volleys) or drop-kicks as before and moves to the right cone, etc.

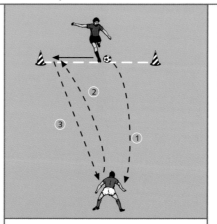

FOCUS ON

• punt: taking a few short steps and throwing the ball up a short distance with both hands
• drop-kick: stretching both arms out in front of you and dropping the ball, or throwing it up with one hand

VARIATIONS

1. The goalkeeper turns around once completely before touching the cone.
2. After touching the cone, the goalkeeper dives to the side for a shot on the ground.

Multiple Player Technique Training

BASIC EXERCISE 3

Two goalkeepers stand facing each other in six-yard-wide goals, 15 yards apart. They have one ball, which they punt (or volley) or drop-kick back and forth.

FOCUS ON (DROP-KICK)
- raising the knee of the kicking leg (the foot meets the ball below knee level)
- a quick, short movement toward the ball (kicking leg does not swing through)
- keeping the ankle firm and toes pointing downward

VARIATIONS
1. The receiver shows at the left or right "post" and receives a precise pass from the other goalkeeper.
2. The goalkeepers pass two balls simultaneously.
3. One goalkeeper always punts (or volleys); the other always drop-kicks. Players switch roles after several rounds.

Exercises on the Goal

BASIC EXERCISE 4

The goalkeeper has a ball and stands behind a five-yard-wide goal; the coach (C) stands at a cone 12 yards in front of it. The goalkeeper punts to C, runs quickly around the goal and stops a ground ball from C aimed at the corner of the goal. Ideally, several goalkeepers should take part in this exercise.

FOCUS ON (PUNTING)
- swinging the kicking leg forward and hitting the ball with the full instep
- fluid movements: after kicking the ball, swinging the leg through in the direction of the kick and taking an extra step

VARIATIONS
1. An extra goalkeeper stands in the goal. C catches GK1's punt and passes it to a cone. GK1 runs around the goal. GK2 runs to the ball at the cone, picks it up and tries to score with a well-aimed punt or drop-kick before GK1 can get oriented.
2. Both goalkeepers do forward rolls before starting for the goal and ball.

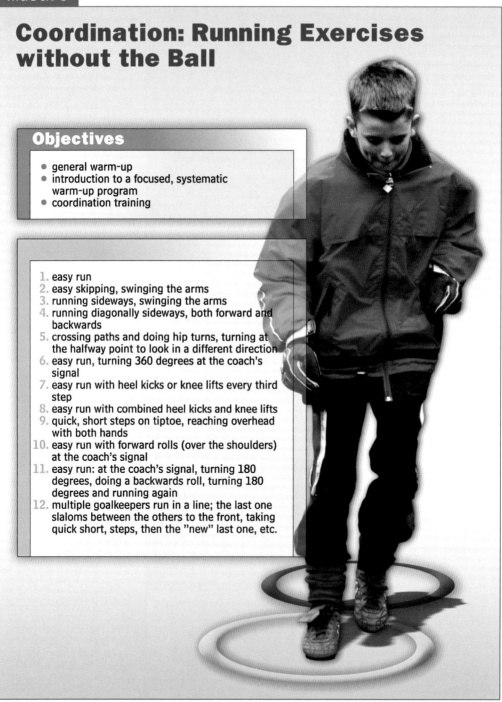

Illustr. 6

Coordination: Running Exercises without the Ball

Objectives

- general warm-up
- introduction to a focused, systematic warm-up program
- coordination training

1. easy run
2. easy skipping, swinging the arms
3. running sideways, swinging the arms
4. running diagonally sideways, both forward and backwards
5. crossing paths and doing hip turns, turning at the halfway point to look in a different direction
6. easy run, turning 360 degrees at the coach's signal
7. easy run with heel kicks or knee lifts every third step
8. easy run with combined heel kicks and knee lifts
9. quick, short steps on tiptoe, reaching overhead with both hands
10. easy run with forward rolls (over the shoulders) at the coach's signal
11. easy run: at the coach's signal, turning 180 degrees, doing a backwards roll, turning 180 degrees and running again
12. multiple goalkeepers run in a line; the last one slaloms between the others to the front, taking quick short, steps, then the "new" last one, etc.

Coordination: Running Exercises without the Ball

EXERCISE 1

Each goalkeeper has a ball and practices alone. The player dribbles for a stretch, then runs the next stretch without the ball, executing coordination exercises as shown in Illustration 6.

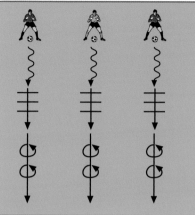

OBJECTIVES
- general warm-up
- coordination training
- teaching technical skills (receiving back passes)

VARIATIONS
1. The player dribbles with the right (or left) foot only.
2. The player alternates dribbling with the insides of the right and left feet.
3. The player takes the ball sideways with the sole of the right (or left) foot.
4. The player dribbles a short distance, then "shuffles" the ball back and forth between both feet, then resumes dribbling.
5. While dribbling, the player kicks the ball ahead a short distance, turns around once completely and resumes dribbling.

EXERCISE 2

Each goalkeeper has a ball and practices alone, taking the ball the entire length of the practice course.
While running, the player bounces the ball with the right and left hands alternately.

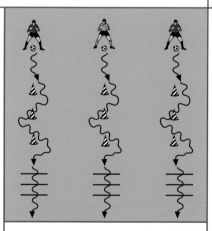

OBJECTIVES
- general warm-up
- motivational warm-up
- coordination training
- goalkeeper-specific technique training
- developing mobility and a feel for the ball

VARIATIONS
1. The player skips, bouncing the ball hard with the right and left hands alternately.
2. The player bounces the ball hard while running, turns around once completely and continues bouncing.
3. The player bounces the ball hard with the right hand, runs under it and then bounces it with the left hand (constantly changing sides and hands).
4. While walking, the goalkeeper bounces the ball in a figure eight around and between the legs (alternating hands).

EXERCISE 3

Each goalkeeper has a ball and practices alone, taking the ball the entire length of the practice course.
While walking, the goalkeeper bounces the ball in a figure eight around and between the legs. At the coach's signal, the player stops with legs apart, rolls the ball between them from behind with both hands and dives forward after the ball (rolling and diving a different direction each time).

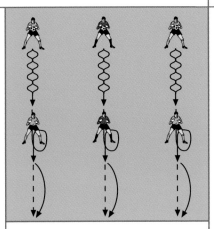

OBJECTIVES
- See Exercise 2

VARIATION

The player takes a short lunge step forward, rolls the ball with the right (or left) hand between the legs from the right (or left) and dives to the left (or right).

EXERCISE 4

Each goalkeeper has a ball and practices alone, taking the ball the entire length of the practice course.
While running, the goalkeeper holds the ball at hip height and passes it around the body, alternately clockwise and counterclockwise.

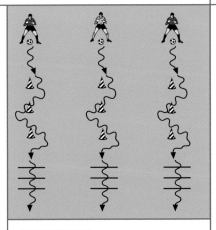

OBJECTIVES
- See Exercise 2

VARIATIONS

1. The player passes the ball around the body once, then throws it overhead from one hand to the other and starts over again.
2. While running, the player bounces the ball up in the air with the knee (alternating between the left knee and the right) and catches it.
3. While running, the player kicks the ball up in the air (alternating between the left foot and the right) and catches it.

EXERCISE 5

Two goalkeepers practice together; each has a ball. They run side by side, and at the coach's signal each throws simultaneously to the other (one high, one low).

OBJECTIVES
• See Exercise 2

VARIATIONS

1. Sequence is the same, except the goalkeepers run sideways.
2. Two goalkeepers run side by side, and at the coach's signal they bounce their balls hard on the ground and quickly trade places.

EXERCISE 6

Two goalkeepers practice together; each has a ball. One runs after the other. At the coach's signal, the player in front bounces the ball hard on the ground and sprints forward. The second player immediately throws the other ball in an arc over the first player's head. Each moves to catch the other's ball and secure it as quickly as possible.

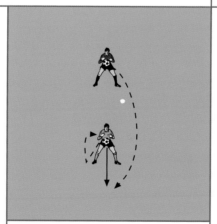

OBJECTIVES
• See Exercise 2

VARIATIONS

1. Make the distance between the goalkeepers a little greater. The player in front stands with legs apart and bounces the ball back between them, and the other one throws the other ball in an arc over the first player's head. Each tries to secure the other's ball as quickly as possible.
2. The player in front throws the ball straight up, and the other one immediately reacts by throwing the other ball forward over the first player's head. Each tries to secure the other's ball as quickly as possible.

Running Exercises with Ball and Coach

EXERCISE 1

Two goalkeepers practice with the coach (C); each goal-keeper has a ball.
C runs between the goal-keepers. At C's signal, one goalkeeper throws to C.
C throws a high ball to one side, and the goalkeeper runs to catch it in the air.

OBJECTIVES
• general warm-up
• motivational warm-up
• coordination training
• goalkeeper-specific technique training
• developing mobility and a feel for the ball

VARIATIONS
1. The goalkeeper throws the ball to C, then turns around once completely before catching it (C waits a moment before throwing it back, so the player has time to turn around).
2. The goalkeeper has to do a forward roll before catching the ball.

EXERCISE 2

Setup is the same as Exercise 1. At an audible signal from the coach, both goalkeepers run forward and throw their balls up into the middle; then each one switches sides and catches the other one's ball in the air.
Note: Running paths should be determined in advance to keep players from running into each other. The throws must be timed perfectly. If this exercise is too demand-ing, try it with just one ball at first.
"Go!"

OBJECTIVES
• See Exercise 1

VARIATIONS
1. One goalkeeper throws the ball up in the air; the other bounces it hard on the ground.
2. One goalkeeper throws the ball up in the air; the other drops it.

EXERCISE 3

Setup is as above; at the coach's signal, both goal-keepers simultaneously roll their balls straight ahead. Each one quickly switches sides (paths determined in advance) and dives for the other one's ball (the one coming from the right dives to the right; the other dives to the left).

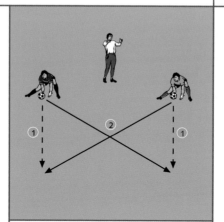

VARIATION

Before diving for the ball, each goalkeeper has to do a coordination exercise (turn around once completely, do a forward roll, etc.).

OBJECTIVES
• See Exercise 1

EXERCISE 4

Two goalkeepers practice with the coach (C). One player runs after the other; C has a ball and stands off to one side. At C's signal, the player in front stops with legs apart; the other player crawls between them and dives for a ground ball from C. Afterwards the two players switch roles.

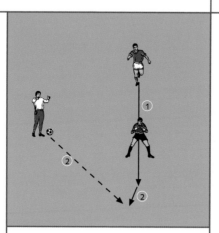

VARIATIONS

1. Sequence is the same as above, except the goalkeeper has to do a forward roll before diving for the ball.
2. At C's signal, the player in front (GK1) stops and squats. GK2 jumps over GK1 and catches a high ball thrown from the side by C.

OBJECTIVES
• See Exercise 1

Game 1

EXERCISE 1

Two goalkeepers practice together in a 10 x 10-yard field (four goalkeepers would be an ideal group size). The field is divided into two halves by two or three two-yard-wide goals in the middle. Each goalkeeper has a ball. One goalkeeper from each pair stands in the left half, the other in the right. Goalkeepers dribble inside the field without leaving it or bumping into each other. At the coach's signal, they pass through the goals, receive their partners' passes and continue dribbling.

OBJECTIVES

- motivational warm-up
- coordination training
- technique training (general and goalkeeper-specific)
- developing mobility and a feel for the ball

VARIATIONS

1. Goalkeepers pass to their partners as follows: They dribble toward each other and stop their balls in the same goal; then each immediately starts dribbling the other's ball into the other half. They use eye contact to agree on a goal.
2. Goalkeepers pass through the same goal (communicate!), run around it and continue dribbling their own balls into the other half.

EXERCISE 2

Setup is as above. Goalkeepers bounce their balls, alternating between the left hand and the right. At the coach's signal, they bounce their balls hard on the ground, run to the other half through any goal and secure their partners' balls against their bodies as quickly as possible.

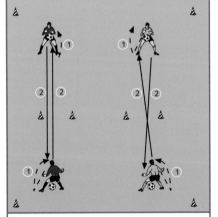

OBJECTIVES

- See Exercise 1

VARIATION

Each goalkeeper has to do a coordination exercise (turn around once completely, do a forward roll, etc.) before switching halves.

Game 2

EXERCISE 1

Several goalkeepers move about a 10 x 10-yard field; each has a ball. The field is divided into halves by a small goal (two yards wide) in the middle.

The goalkeepers dribble. The coach calls a name, and that player kicks a precise pass to the coach, runs sideways through the goal and dives to stop the coach's ground ball.

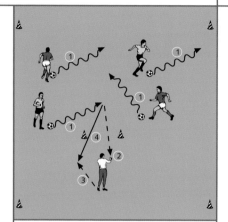

VARIATION

Each goalkeeper has to do a coordination exercise before diving for the ball (turn around once completely, do a forward roll, lie face-down, run around a cone, etc.).

OBJECTIVES

- motivational warm-up
- coordination training
- technique training (general and goal-keeper-specific)
- developing mobility and a feel for the ball

EXERCISE 2

Setup is as above. Goalkeepers dribble inside a field half without leaving it or bumping into each other. At the coach's signal, they all dribble through the goal into the other half, etc.

VARIATIONS

1. At the coach's signal, the goalkeepers pass through the goal, turn around once completely and run to retrieve their balls in the other half.
2. Goalkeepers do forward rolls before retrieving their balls.

OBJECTIVES

- See Exercise 1

EXERCISE 3

Setup is as above. Goalkeepers dribble inside a field half without leaving it or bumping into each other. At the coach's signal, they stop their balls, run through the goal into the other half, do forward rolls, run back through the goal to different balls and resume dribbling.

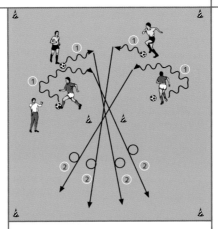

OBJECTIVES
• See Exercise 1

VARIATION

Competition: One goalkeeper has no ball. When the goalkeepers return from the other half, which one is left without a ball?

Game 3

EXERCISE 1

Two goalkeepers practice together in a 10 x 10-yard field (four goalkeepers would be an ideal group size). Each goalkeeper has a ball. Goalkeepers bounce their balls while running, alternating between the left hand and the right, and passing frequently to their partners.

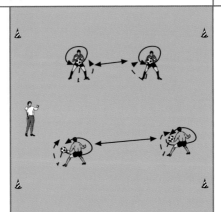

OBJECTIVES
• motivational warm-up
• coordination training
• technique training (general and goalkeeper-specific)
• developing mobility and a feel for the ball

VARIATIONS

1. Goalkeepers throw to their partners.
2. After trading balls, goalkeepers roll them a short distance ahead and dive after them. (Note: Alternate between diving to the left and to the right.)
3. Before diving for the ball, each goalkeeper does a coordination exercise (turn around once completely, do a forward roll, etc.).

EXERCISE 2

Setup is as above.
While running, goalkeepers pass their balls around their bodies at hip level. At the coach's signal, they bounce the balls hard on the ground, run to their partners' balls and secure them against their bodies as quickly as possible. Running paths are determined in advance.

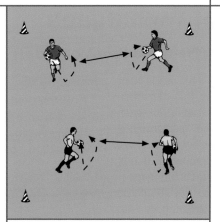

OBJECTIVES
• See Exercise 1

VARIATIONS

1. Goalkeepers bounce their balls forward between their legs, run to their partners' balls and secure them against their bodies as quickly as possible.
2. Goalkeepers throw their balls up in the air, run to their partners' balls and try to catch them in the air.

Practical Exercises for Individual Techniques

Catching Low Balls (from the Front or Side)

Once goalkeepers at this age level have mastered the basic techniques, they can move on to more challenging exercises. For each technique described in the performance profile, we have included three basic exercises, which can be changed and combined with one another. We advise against practicing individual techniques by themselves; they should be combined with coordination training or with other goalkeeper-specific techniques.

Basic tactics like positional play, set plays, attack building, 1 v. 1 play and winning the ball are always addressed in the third basic exercise. You should also start focusing more on these tactics in your general team training sessions.

REMEMBER:

Coordination training should never be separate; it's always better to do it during warm-up in combination with technique exercises.

On all exercises on the goal, place a cone in the center of the goal for easier orientation.

Technique and Coordination

BASIC EXERCISE 1A

The goalkeeper stands in front of the left post of a three-yard-wide goal. The coach (C) has a ball and stands five yards in front of the goal. C kicks a low shot in the air. The goalkeeper catches it and throws it back to C, turns around once completely, moving to the right, and assumes the basic position in front of the right post. C shoots at that post, the goalkeeper catches it, etc.

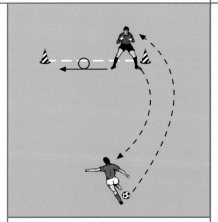

VARIATIONS

1. After turning around, the goalkeeper runs quickly around the cone before resuming the basic position.
2. The goalkeeper turns halfway around, stops facing away from the post, runs backwards around it and then assumes the basic position.

FOCUS ON
- taking a short step toward the ball, bending slightly forward from the waist
- reaching for the ball with both hands, arms almost completely extended
- keeping the elbows as close together as possible

BASIC EXERCISE 1B

The goalkeeper sits two yards in front of a three-yard-wide goal. The coach (C) has a ball and stands five yards in front of the goal. At C's signal, the goalkeeper does a backwards roll, stands up quickly (without using hands), assumes the basic position and catches a low ball from C. Then the goalkeeper throws the ball back to C, does a forward roll and sits in front of the goal again.

FOCUS ON
- See Exercise 1A

VARIATIONS

1. While kneeling, the goalkeeper catches a low ball from C and throws it back, then catches a second shot off to one side, secures it, rolls onto his side and pushes himself back up with his elbow, keeping the ball secured against his body throughout the roll.
2. The goalkeeper catches a low ball from C, then does a sideways roll as above, but from a standing position.

Multiple Player Technique Training

BASIC EXERCISE 2A

Two goalkeepers stand facing each other, 10 yards apart. Each stands in the middle of a seven-yard-wide goal. Another cone stands two yards behind each goalkeeper. GK1 throws a ball one-handed, underhand so that GK2 can catch it between hip and chest level. Then GK2 throws to GK1, etc.

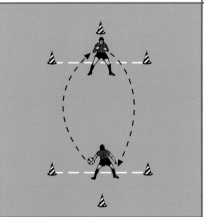

FOCUS ON
- absorbing the ball's momentum with hands and upper arms
- bending the upper body over the ball and wrapping the hands around it

VARIATION

The coach (C) has a ball and stands between the goals, five yards off to one side. GK1 throws to GK2, then turns toward C, assumes the basic position and catches a low ball from the side from C. GK1 throws it back to C, turns toward GK2 and assumes the basic position. GK2 throws a low ball to GK1, turns toward C, assumes the basic position and catches a low ball from the side from C, etc.

BASIC EXERCISE 2B

Setup is as above.
GK1 passes on the ground to GK2 with the inside of the foot, turns toward the coach (C), assumes the basic position and catches a low ball from the side from C. GK2 receives GK1's ball and "shuffles" it from foot to foot until GK1 throws back to C. Then GK2 passes to GK1, turns toward C, assumes the basic position and catches a low ball from the side from C. Now GK1 shuffles the ball from foot to foot, etc.

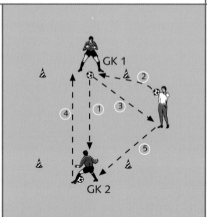

FOCUS ON
• See Exercise 2A

VARIATIONS

1. C throws high balls from the side, which the goalkeepers catch and throw back.
2. C passes on the ground, and the goalkeepers pass back directly.

Exercises on the Goal

BASIC EXERCISE 3A

The goalkeeper stands in the middle of a standard goal. The coach (C) has two balls and stands 10 yards in front of the goal. C holds one ball and stands behind another. C drop-kicks the first one (low) at the goalkeeper, who catches it and throws it back to C. Then C shoots the second ball on the ground, to one side of the goalkeeper.

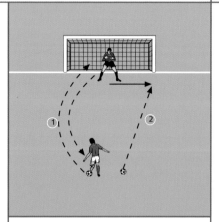

FOCUS ON
• taking a short step toward the ball, bending slightly forward from the waist
• rolling over the hips, side and shoulder

VARIATIONS

1. C throws the second ball high and straight at the goalkeeper, who catches it and throws it back to C.
2. A second goalkeeper (GK2) stands 15 yards in front of the goal. GK1 catches the first ball and rolls it to GK2, who tries to score with a well-aimed instep shot. Goalkeepers switch roles and positions if GK2 scores, or after several rounds.
3. GK2 shoots on the ground with the inside of the foot.

BASIC EXERCISE 3B

Using two cones, divide the goal box line in front of a standard goal into three equal sections (goals). GK1 stands in front of the goal and to the right, GK2 at a cone in the center of the goal. GK2's job is to observe GK1's positional play (on an imaginary line between the ball and the center of the goal). The coach (C) has a ball and stands five yards in front of GK1. C kicks a low ball to GK1, who catches the ball and throws it back to C. Now C and GK1 move left to the next goal, and the exercise starts over again.

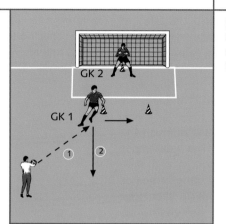

FOCUS ON
- See Exercise 3A

NOTE

GK1 practices twice in each goal, then switches roles and positions with GK2.

BASIC EXERCISE 3C

GK1 stands in the middle of a standard goal, GK2 15 yards in front of it. The coach (C) kicks a low ball from the side to GK1, who catches it and rolls it to GK2. Then GK2 plays 1 v. 1 to score.

FOCUS ON
- See Exercise 3A

VARIATION

GK2 stands 10 yards in front of the goal. C kicks a low ball to GK1, who catches it and drop-kicks it (low) to GK2. Then GK1 immediately turns back toward C, who shoots a second ball on the ground at the near corner. GK1 deflects it to the side and stands up again immediately. Now GK2 tries to score by rolling the ball into the goal.

Catching High Balls (from the Front or Side)

As young goalkeepers reach the 10- to 12-year-old level and make the transition to the big field, catching high balls becomes especially important.

Now is the time for them to refine their technique for catching high balls and adapt it to a larger area.

The goalkeeper's position at the moment the cross is kicked is critical. The goalkeeper assumes the appropriate position and then makes a decision: Do I leave the goal line or not? The goalkeeper's teammates should be informed of the decision as quickly as possible.

It is best for goalkeepers to practice goalkeeper-specific techniques on their own and tactics together with the rest of the team.

Making the Decision:
1. Where is the crosser, and how far away?
2. How long will the ball be in the air?
3. What is the "level of difficulty" on this cross (power, spin, etc.)?

Technique and Coordination

BASIC EXERCISE 1A

Goalkeepers 1 and 2 stand facing each other in five-yard-wide goals, 10 yards apart. The coach (C) has several balls and stands five yards off to one side. At C's signal, both goalkeepers do forward rolls. C throws a high ball to GK1. Meanwhile, GK2 switches to Goal A by running in front of GK1. GK1 catches the ball, throws it back to C and switches to Goal B. Then C throws the GK2, and the exercise starts over again.

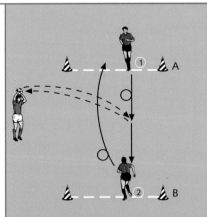

VARIATIONS

1. The goalkeepers stand in the middle between the goals, back to back. At C's signal, they do forward rolls and turn around. C throws a high ball from the side to GK1, who catches it and throws it back to C. The goalkeepers switch sides.
2. Both goalkeepers step quickly to the right and back to the middle; then GK1 catches the ball.

FOCUS ON
- catching the ball as soon as possible, in front of or above the head
- jumping to catch the ball at the highest point possible, with ankle, knee and hip joints fully extended

BASIC EXERCISE 1B

Setup is as above.
Another cone stands three yards in front of each goal. At C's signal, both goalkeepers run forward, touch the cones, turn to face C and run sideways back to their goals. Then C throws a high ball from the side to GK1, who catches it and throws it back to C. The goalkeepers switch sides.

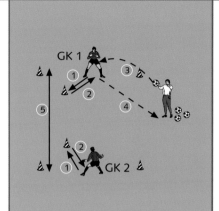

VARIATIONS

1. After touching the cones, both goalkeepers do backwards rolls.
2. The goalkeepers run around the cones, then run backwards back to their goals. C throws a ball from the side to GK1, who catches it and throws it back to C. The goalkeepers switch sides.
3. The goalkeepers do forward rolls before running around the cones.

FOCUS ON
- fluid, integrated movements
- jumping to catch the ball at the highest point possible, with ankle, knee and hip joints fully extended

Multiple Player Technique Training

BASIC EXERCISE 2A

GK1 stands in the center of a five-yard-wide goal, GK2 about six yards in front of it. The coach (C) has a ball and stands six yards off to one side.
C throws a high ball to GK1, who catches it and throws it to GK2. Then GK2 throws a high ball to GK1, who catches it, throws it to C and returns to the center of the goal, etc. Goalkeepers switch roles and positions after several rounds.

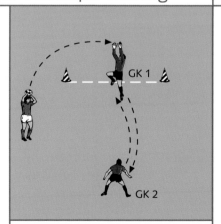

VARIATION

After throwing the ball to C or GK2, GK1 does a backwards roll toward the goal.

FOCUS ON
- keeping your eyes on the ball
- swinging the arms for more momentum on the jump
- extending the arms forward or upward toward the ball

BASIC EXERCISE 2B

Setup is as above.
C and GK2 each have a ball.
GK1 catches a high ball from C, throws it back, faces GK2 and runs sideways back to the goal, then catches a high ball from GK2. GK1 throws the ball back to GK2, faces C and runs sideways back to the goal.

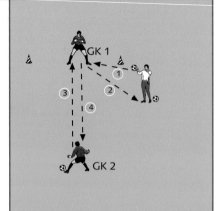

VARIATIONS

1. The goalkeepers crowd each other a little while catching the ball. However, the focus is on catching, not on 1 v. 1 play.
2. GK2 bounces the ball hard toward GK1.

FOCUS ON

- keeping your eyes on the ball
- swinging the arms for more momentum on the jump
- extending the arms forward or upward toward the ball
- taking off with the front foot

Exercises on the Goal

BASIC EXERCISE 3A

GK1 stands in the center of a standard goal. The coach (C) has a ball and stands seven yards in front of the goal. GK2 stands at a cone behind C, on or near the top of the penalty area. C kicks a low ball from the front to GK1, who catches it and throws it back to C. After several shots, C throws a high ball. GK1 catches it and rolls it on the ground to GK2. Then GK2 tries to score with a well-aimed instep shot. Goalkeepers switch roles and positions if GK2 scores, or after several rounds.

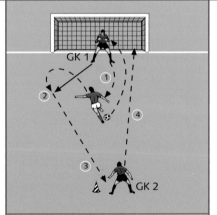

VARIATIONS

1. C interferes while the goal-keeper catches the ball.
2. C bounces the ball hard toward the goalkeeper and interferes while the goal-keeper catches the ball.

FOCUS ON

- wrapping the hands around the ball, fingers spread wide
- bending the elbows at the moment of contact and pulling the ball in to the body
- getting a running start and taking off with one leg

BASIC EXERCISE 3B

GK1 stands in the center of a standard goal as above. The coach (C) stands five yards off to one side. GK2 has a ball and stands at a cone about 12 yards in front of the goal. C throws a high ball to GK1, who catches it and throws it back to C. Then GK1 turns to GK2 and catches a low ball. GK1 throws it back to GK2 and turns toward C again. Goalkeepers switch roles and positions after several rounds.

VARIATION

C throws a high ball to GK1, who tries to catch it while GK2 tries to head it into the goal.

FOCUS ON
● See Exercise 3A

BASIC EXERCISE 3C

Setup is as above. C throws a high ball to GK1, who catches it in the air, then immediately starts running toward GK2, who is running toward the goal. GK1 runs around the cone and then volleys or drop-kicks at the goal. GK2 tries to block the shot. Then C throws a high ball to GK2, etc.

VARIATION

The goalkeepers start from various starting positions (e.g. lying face-down or face-up, push-up position, etc.).

FOCUS ON
● See Exercise 3A

Diving and Rolling Sideways on Ground Balls

Technique and Coordination

BASIC EXERCISE 1A

The goalkeeper stands at a cone. Two yards away, there are three more cones marking two three-yard-wide goals (A and B). The coach (C) has a ball and stands five yards in front of them. At C's signal ("A" or "B"), the goalkeeper runs around the center cone and stops a ground ball from C in the designated goal. The center cone is a bit behind the other two, so that the goalkeeper has to move forward to the ball.

VARIATION

The goalkeeper does a forward roll before running around the center cone.

FOCUS ON

- rolling over the hips, side and shoulder
- "stopping the ball out in front": on a ball to the right, taking a short step toward it with the right foot and stopping it as soon as possible

BASIC EXERCISE 1B

The goalkeeper stands at a cone, three yards behind another cone. The coach (C) has a ball and stands three yards in front of the second cone. Two five-yard-wide goals (A and B) are marked between the two cones, about two yards apart. At C's signal, the goalkeeper runs to the cone in front, touches it, runs backwards to the rear cone and moves to block a ground ball from C in the designated goal.

VARIATIONS

1. The goalkeeper does a forward roll before running to the front cone.
2. After touching the front cone, the goalkeeper does a backwards roll.
3. The goalkeeper starts from various starting positions.

FOCUS ON
• See Exercise 1A

Multiple Player Technique Training

BASIC EXERCISE 2A

GK1 stands in the center of a six-yard-wide goal. GK2 crouches just to the right of GK1, and the coach (C) has a ball and stands five yards in front of GK1. At C's signal, GK1 runs backwards around GK2, jumps over GK2 (taking off with the rear leg) and dives to the side for a ground ball from C. Goalkeepers switch roles and positions after several rounds (practice on both sides!).

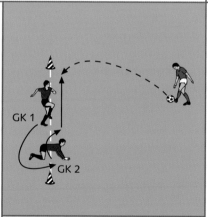

VARIATIONS

1. GK2 is in push-up position. GK1 runs backwards around GK2, crawls under GK2 and dives for a ground ball from C.
2. GK1 crawls under GK2, jumps over GK2 and proceeds as above.

FOCUS ON
• securing the ball against the body
• keeping the elbows in front of the body
• moving sideways before falling on the ball

BASIC EXERCISE 2B

Two goalkeepers practice together. GK1 lays face-up in the center of a six-yard wide goal, head toward the coach (C). C has a ball and stands five yards in front of the goal. GK2 has a ball and stands three yards to C's right. At C's signal, GK1 rolls over to the right, gets up quickly and passes a ground ball directly back to GK2 with the inside of the left foot. Then GK1 dives to the right for a ground ball from C.

FOCUS ON
- keeping the elbows in front of the body
- securing the ball against the body

VARIATIONS
1. GK2 throws a low ball to GK1, who volleys it back.
2. GK1 stops one ground ball from GK2 on the left side and another from C on the right.

Exercises on the Goal

BASIC EXERCISE 3A

GK1 stands in a standard goal; C has a ball and stands five yards away from the right corner. GK2 stands two yards in front of the left corner of the penalty box, and GK3 has a ball and stands at the right goal box corner (both at cones). C throws a high ball to GK1, who catches it and rolls it to GK2. At the same moment, GK3 kicks a ground ball at the right corner of the goal. GK1 stops it, stands up and dives to the other corner for another ball from GK2. Goalkeepers rotate clockwise every three rounds.

FOCUS ON
- reaching for the ball with both hands
- keeping your eyes on the ball

VARIATION
GK1 stands at the right post facing C. C passes on the ground, and GK1 dives to the left and deflects the ball to GK3, then stands up quickly and dives to the left corner for a ball from GK2. Then GK3 shoots at the right corner.

BASIC EXERCISE 3B

GK1 is in push-up position (-legs apart) six yards in front of the goal. The coach (C) has several balls and stands behind GK1. GK2 stands to the left of the goal at a cone. C passes under GK1 toward the goal. GK1 stands up quickly and deflects the ball with the left hand to GK2, then stands up again, turns around and dives to the right for another ground ball from C. Goalkeepers switch roles and positions after several rounds (practice on both sides).

FOCUS ON
• See Exercise 3A

VARIATION

A third goalkeeper (GK3) has a ball and stands behind C and to the right, on or near the top of the penalty box. After GK1 deflects the first ball to GK2, GK3 tries to score with a well-aimed instep shot. Goalkeepers switch roles and positions after each round.

BASIC EXERCISE 3C

GK1 stands in a standard goal with a five-yard-wide goal 16 yards in front of it. The coach (C) has a ball and stands five yards in front of the smaller goal. GK2 stands at the left post of the small goal. C shoots on the ground at the far corner of this goal, and GK2 dives for the ball, stands up quickly, turns around, kicks the ball a short distance ahead and then tries to score against GK1 with a well-aimed instep shot. Goalkeepers switch roles and positions if GK2 scores, or after several rounds.

FOCUS ON
• See Exercise 3A

VARIATIONS

1. Both goalkeepers lie on their backs. At C's first signal, GK2 rolls over and stands up quickly, then dives for a ball on the side. At C's second signal, GK1 rolls over, stands up quickly and assumes the basic position in the center of the goal. GK2 then tries to score with an instep kick.
2. GK2 drop-kicks or volleys (instead of the instep shot).

Throwing, Kicking, Punting, Drop-Kicking

Technique and Coordination

BASIC EXERCISE 1A

The goalkeeper has a ball and stands in a five-yard-wide goal with a cone two yards in front of it. The coach (C) stands five yards in front of the cone. The goalkeeper throws the ball to C, runs around the cone and back to the goal, and turns to face C. C kicks a high volley to the goalkeeper, who catches it and volleys back to C. Then the sequence starts over, except this time C drop-kicks to the goalkeeper, who catches the ball, drop-kicks it back and runs around the cone and back to the goal.

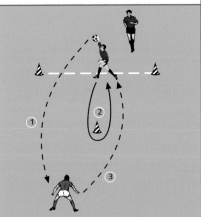

FOCUS ON (THROWING)

- "opening" the upper body, swinging one arm quickly forward and bringing the throwing arm forward immediately afterwards
- keeping the hand on the ball and, more importantly, behind it as long as possible

VARIATIONS

1. The goalkeeper has to run a complete circle around the cone.
2. The goalkeeper starts the exercise with a forward roll.
3. The goalkeeper runs sideways back to the goal.
4. The goalkeeper runs around the cone, does a forward roll and runs backwards back to the goal.

BASIC EXERCISE 1B

Starting positions are the same as in Exercise 1A, except now the cone is four yards in front of the goal, and C stands six yards in front of the cone. The goalkeeper throws the ball to C, runs to the cone and catches a high ball from C there, then runs sideways back to the goal, carrying the ball, and punts or drop-kicks to C. Then the exercise starts over again.

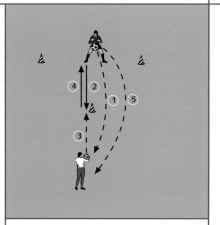

VARIATION

The goalkeeper kicks the first ball to C, does a forward roll and runs to the cone, receives a ground ball from C there and dribbles back to the goal and repositions the ball; then the exercise starts over again.

NOTE

• Both C and the goalkeeper should use a different technique for every pass.

Multiple Player Technique Training

BASIC EXERCISE 2A

Four goalkeepers practice together. GK1 (who has a ball) and GK2 line up in a five-yard-wide goal (A). GK3 and GK4 stand 10 yards in front of them in another goal (B). GK1 throws the ball to GK3, who catches it and throws it back. GK1 then drop-kicks to GK3 and runs to Goal B. GK3 catches the ball, drop-kicks it to GK2 and runs to Goal A. GK2 catches the ball and throws it to GK4. GK4 catches it and throws it back to GK2, who drop-kicks it to GK4 and runs to Goal B, etc.

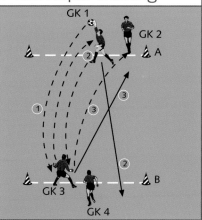

VARIATIONS

1. Goalkeepers do forward rolls before switching sides.
2. Goalkeepers do backwards rolls halfway across the field, then run backwards the rest of the way to the other goal.

FOCUS ON (DROP-KICK)

• keeping the ankle firm and the toes pointing downward
• pointing the toes of the plant foot in the direction of the kick
• placing the standing leg even with the ball

BASIC EXERCISE 2B

Setup is as above, except now GK3 and GK4 stand 20 yards away from Goal A.

GK1 kicks a high ball to GK3, who stops it like a back pass and then kicks a high ball back. GK1 catches the ball, drop-kicks it back to GK3 and runs to Goal B. GK3 catches the ball in front of his body, drop-kicks it to GK2 and runs to Goal A. GK2 catches the ball in front of his body and drop-kicks to GK4, who catches it and drop-kicks it back to GK2. GK2 stops it like a back pass, kicks it back to GK4 and runs to Goal B. GK4 stops the ball and kicks it to GK3 in Goal A, and the exercise starts over again.

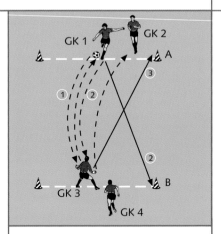

FOCUS ON (DROP-KICK)
- See Exercise 2A

Exercises on the Goal

BASIC EXERCISE 3A

Three goalkeepers practice together. GK1 stands in a standard goal, GK2 has a ball and stands on the goal line right next to the goal, and GK3 stands at a cone 15 yards in front of the goal. GK2 sets the ball on the line and kicks it to GK3, who catches it and then tries to score with a well-aimed drop-kick. Goalkeepers switch roles and positions if GK3 scores, or after several rounds.

FOCUS ON (KICKING)
- keeping the plant leg behind or next to the ball
- approaching the ball diagonally
- hitting the ball squarely in the middle
- letting the kicking leg swing through the kick (follow through)

VARIATIONS

1. Instead of catching the ball, GK3 receives it like a back pass.
2. GK2 uses different passing techniques. GK3 has to try to score with whatever technique GK2 uses.
3. GK2 stands at the right corner of the penalty box and kicks a high ball to GK1. GK1 catches it and throws it to GK3, who receives it like a back pass and then tries to score with an instep kick.

BASIC EXERCISE 3B

The coach (C) has a ball and stands at the corner of the goal box. A ball is placed at the center of the goal box line. GK1 stands in the goal, GK2 and GK3 at cones about 16 yards away. C throws a high ball over GK1's head toward the far post. GK1 catches the ball and throws it to GK3, who catches it. Then GK1 kicks the ball on the goal box line to GK2, who receives it. GK3 tries to score with a drop-kick, and then GK2 does the same.

FOCUS ON (KICKING)
* See Exercise 3A

BASIC EXERCISE 3C

Setup is as above.
The coach (C) throws a high ball toward the far post; GK1 throws it back and then kicks the ball on the goal box line to GK2. C passes on the ground to GK3, who shoots directly.

FOCUS ON (PUNTING)
* taking a few steps and then throwing the ball up a short distance with both hands
* hitting the ball with the full instep and letting the kicking leg swing through the kick (follow through)

Sample Practice Session, Part 1

The following exercises make up a fun practice session that your players are sure to enjoy!

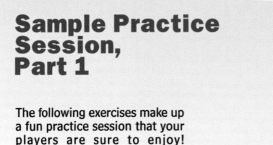

Setup

Practice Time:	50-60 minutes
Group Size:	three or four goalkeepers
Equipment:	six balls, one standard goal, cones or other markers
Focus On:	basic position
	catching low balls from the front
	catching high crosses
	falling and rolling sideways on ground balls
	drop-kick
	general technical skills (receiving back passes)

Practice Session

Warm-Up:	See the section on "Coordination Exercises with the Ball" in this chapter.
Practice Time:	15-20 minutes

Technique Training

- **Note:** Do not practice the basic position by itself. Instead, watch for the correct position on every exercise.

Catching Low Balls from the Front

EXERCISE 1

Two goalkeepers stand in five-yard-wide goals, 10 yards apart. GK1 rolls a ground ball to GK2's right (or left) foot, and GK2 kicks a low direct pass back to GK1. GK1 catches it and rolls it back to GK2, who passes it back with the left (or right) foot this time. Goalkeepers switch roles after several rounds.

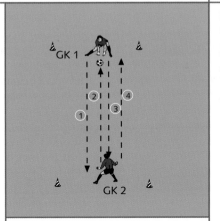

EXERCISE 2

Setup is the same as Exercise 1.
The goalkeepers drop-kick the ball back and forth; after passing, each one turns around once completely (to the left or to the right).

NOTE
* These exercises also improve goal-keeping technique in general (receiving back passes).

Catching High Crosses

Using cones, mark out a lane two or three yards long. The goalkeeper stands in front of it, and the coach has a ball and stands five yards off to the side. The goalkeeper catches a high ball from the left (or right) after executing the following running exercise: run forward on the right side of the lane, backwards in the lane, and forward on the left side.

NOTE
* jumping correctly, taking off with the left leg if the ball is coming from the left (and vice versa)
* fluid, integrated movements
* taking off with the front foot

Diving and Rolling Sideways on Ground Balls

EXERCISE 1

The goalkeeper stands in a six-yard-wide goal. The coach (C) has a ball and stands five yards in front of the goal. C throws the ball to the left of the goalkeeper, who takes a few short steps to the sides and dives to catch it. While still on the ground, the goalkeeper extends both arms and rolls the ball to C, then stands up, touches the left cone, takes a few steps to the right and dives on another ground ball.

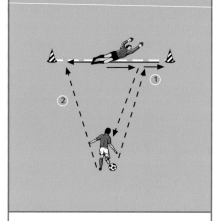

EXERCISE 2

The goalkeeper is in push-up position five yards in front of a small goal. C has two balls and stands directly in front of the goalkeeper. C kicks the first ball under the goalkeeper toward the left side of the goal. The goalkeeper stands up quickly, dives and tries to deflect the ball to the left side with the right hand. Then C kicks another ground ball at the left corner of the goal.

NOTE
- two plays in quick succession
- moving sideways before diving for the second ball

Illustr. 8

Sample Practice Session, Part 2

Drop-Kick

See the exercises for catching low balls from the front in this chapter.

General Technical Skills

Receiving back passes:
See the exercises for catching low balls from the front in this chapter.

Playing time: 15 to 20 minutes

2 or 4 Goalkeepers on Two Goals

EXERCISE 1

Set up a standard goal and a five-yard-wide goal facing each other, 15 yards apart, with a goalkeeper in each. Another goalkeeper waits behind each goal. The coach stands on an imaginary centerline and either throws a high ball to GK1 or drop-kicks it to GK2. GK1 catches the ball and tries to score on the small goal with a well-aimed throw. GK2 tries to score on the standard goal with a drop-kick. Goalkeepers switch positions with their partners after each round.

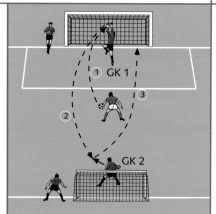

FOCUS ON
* combining techniques: catching low balls from the front, throwing and drop-kicking

VARIATION

After catching the ball, GK1 rolls it a short distance to the side and tries to score with an instep kick. GK2 catches the ball and then plays 1 v. 1 to score.

(The two exercises on this page, combined, should last 15 to 20 minutes.)

EXERCISE 2

GK1 stands in a standard goal. The coach (C) stands four yards in front of the goal, GK2 on the top of the penalty box; each has a ball. C and GK1 kick direct ground balls back and forth; C passes to both of GK1's feet. Suddenly C kicks the ball to one side of GK1, who dives for it, rolls it back while still on the ground, gets up and dives to the other side for a second ball from GK2. GK2 is allowed to shoot as soon as GK1 dives for C's ball. C stays between them to block GK1's view. If GK2 scores, the two goalkeepers switch positions.

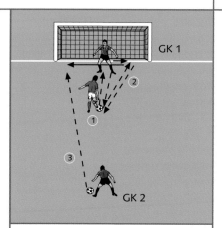

FOCUS ON
* combining the following techniques: diving for ground balls, drop-kicking, throwing and general technical skills (preparation for the back pass rule)

VARIATION

GK2 drop-kicks or throws the ball.

(The two exercises on this page, combined, should last 15 to 20 minutes.)

Moving On: Intermediate Training with 12- to 14-Year-Olds

Training 12- to 14-Year-Olds

The optimal training program for goalkeepers at this age level is significantly different from what it was at the previous one, even though both belong to the "intermediate training" phase. Below are some important rules and guidelines to keep in mind as you work with your players.

• Ages 12 through 14 mark the first stage of puberty, which is the best time to work on all aspects of condition.

• Hormonal changes lead to radical changes in players' trainability and their tolerance for intense physical activity.

• Practice should focus primarily on improving condition, and also on stabilizing coordination and improving it as much as possible. Sessions should become longer and more intense. Series include more repetitions than they did at the previous age level.

• The musculature develops the ability to become supersaturated with oxygen in response to activities requiring speed, power and endurance.

• However, strength and endurance exercises should not be too intense. Be careful: Rapid gains in height make the skeletal system more vulnerable to damage from exercises that are too intense, too long or too frequent.

• The passive musculature, especially the spinal muscles, must be protected from overexertion with the help of focused strength training. Strength training should always be carefully monitored – never overdo it!

• Introduce techniques that are dynamic and require increased power, such as diving and jumping for balls in the air. However, keep in mind that as players go through their "second growth" and experience growth spurts of up to three inches per year, you can expect to deal with periods of motor instability and faulty coordina-

tion. This will periodically reduce their ability to learn new techniques. Fortunately, with continuous training, they should be able to maintain the techniques they have already learned.

• Use repetitions to help players internalize previously learned techniques.

• Practice combining the various techniques.

• Address mistakes and make corrections.

• The ability to think abstractly and make mental combinations continues to develop (the development of a „conscious game experience").

• Work on integrating tactics training into full-team practice sessions, taking small groups aside as necessary (e.g. 2 v. 2 following a cross, 3 v. 2 on a goal with goalkeeper, etc.).

• The demands of goalkeeping in actual match play – recognizing situations as they develop (anticipation), moving out from the goal line, etc. – can only be simulated with the help of the rest of the team.

• Players are now becoming interested in social contacts (friends, dating) and new hobbies. Their developing personalities need your recognition and appreciation.

Illustr. 9a

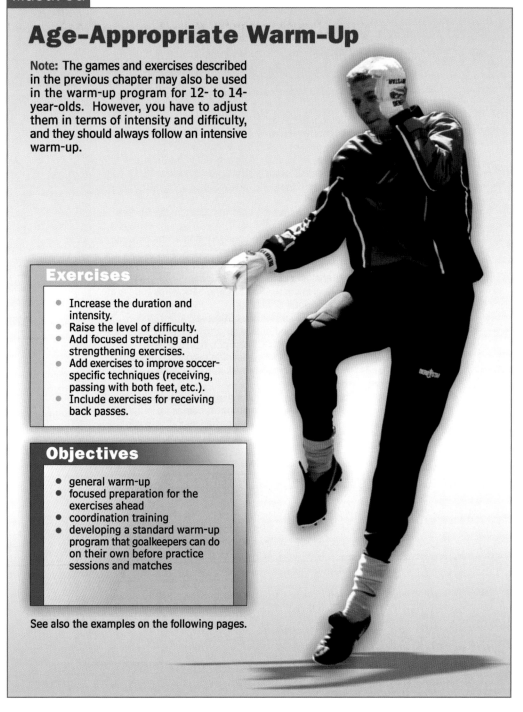

Age-Appropriate Warm-Up

Note: The games and exercises described in the previous chapter may also be used in the warm-up program for 12- to 14-year-olds. However, you have to adjust them in terms of intensity and difficulty, and they should always follow an intensive warm-up.

Exercises

- Increase the duration and intensity.
- Raise the level of difficulty.
- Add focused stretching and strengthening exercises.
- Add exercises to improve soccer-specific techniques (receiving, passing with both feet, etc.).
- Include exercises for receiving back passes.

Objectives

- general warm-up
- focused preparation for the exercises ahead
- coordination training
- developing a standard warm-up program that goalkeepers can do on their own before practice sessions and matches

See also the examples on the following pages.

Illustr. 9b

Warm-Up with 12- to 14-year-old Goalkeepers

Coordination: Running Exercises with the Ball

1. easy run
2. easy run, swinging the arms
3. skipping with arm circles
4. running sideways, swinging the arms
5. running sideways while constantly turning the head
6. running sideways diagonally forward and backwards
7. running sideways diagonally forward, doing forward rolls at the coach's signal
8. running sideways diagonally backwards, doing backwards rolls at the coach's signal
9. crossing paths and doing hip turns, turning at the halfway point to look in a different direction
10. easy run, turning around once completely (alternately to the right and to the left) at the coach's signal
11. easy run with arm circles forward and backwards (one arm, both arms, in various directions)
12. easy run with heel kicks or knee lifts every third step
13. easy run with combined heel kicks and knee lifts (e.g. knee lift right, knee lift left, heel kick right, heel kick left)
14. quick, short steps on tiptoe, reaching overhead with both hands (continually alternating with normal jogging); impetus comes from the toes
15. quick, short steps with legs extended, arms extended forward and fingertips pointing down; impetus comes from the toes
16. continuous knee lifts with knees turned slightly outward; hands in front of the body, palms down; feet (or heels) come up to meet hands
17. continuous knee lifts with knees turned slightly inward; hands extended out to the sides; feet come up to meet hands
18. easy run with forward rolls (over the shoulders) at the coach's signal
19. easy run: at the coach's signal, turning 180 degrees, doing a backwards roll, turning 180 degrees and running again
20. multiple goalkeepers run in a line; the last one slaloms between the others to the front, taking quick short, steps, then the "new" last one, etc.

Coordination Exercises with the Ball

EXERCISE 1

Each goalkeeper has a ball and practices alone. This exercise focuses on improving soccer technique in general and developing mobility and a feel for the ball.

The goalkeeper alternates between the left foot and the right (taking the ball sideways with the left or right sole).

OBJECTIVES
- general warm-up
- coordination training
- developing mobility and a feel for the ball
- general technique training

VARIATIONS

1. The goalkeeper dribbles a short distance, then "shuffles" the ball back and forth between both feet, then resumes dribbling.
2. While dribbling, the player kicks the ball ahead a short distance, turns around once completely and resumes dribbling.
3. While dribbling, the player does a forward roll and resumes dribbling.

EXERCISE 2

Setup is as above. This exercise helps to develop mobility, a feel for the ball and coordination in general. The goalkeeper bounces the ball while running, alternating between the left hand and the right.

OBJECTIVES
- See Exercise 1

VARIATIONS

1. The goalkeeper bounces the ball while skipping, alternating between the left hand and the right.
2. The goalkeeper bounces the ball hard while running, turns around once completely and resumes bouncing.
3. The goalkeeper does a forward roll, then resumes bouncing.

Coordination Exercises in Pairs

EXERCISE 1

Two goalkeepers practice together; each has a ball. They bounce their balls while running side by side; suddenly they trade places and balls. To prevent collisions, they agree in advance that one will run in front, the other behind.

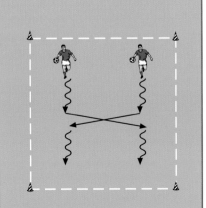

VARIATION

Goalkeepers have to do a coordination exercise (turn around, forward roll, backwards roll etc.) before trading places.

OBJECTIVES

- motivational warm-up
- coordination training
- developing mobility and a feel for the ball
- general and goalkeeper-specific technique training

EXERCISE 2

Setup is as above. Goalkeepers run facing each other (GK1 backwards). At the coach's signal, GK1 bounces one ball hard on the ground, and GK2 throws the other in an arc over GK1's head. Each runs to the other's ball and tries to secure it as quickly as possible (GK1 must turn around first).

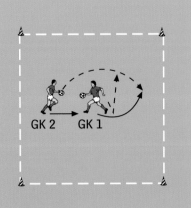

GK 2   GK 1

VARIATIONS

1. Increase the distance between the goalkeepers. GK1 bounces his ball between his legs and behind, and GK2 throws the other in an arc as above. Each tries to secure the other's ball as quickly as possible.
2. GK1 throws his ball back over his head, and GK2 reacts immediately and throws the other in an arc as above. Each tries to secure the other's ball as quickly as possible.

OBJECTIVES

- See Exercise 1

EXERCISE 3

Setup is as above.
The goalkeepers run side by side, throwing their balls back and forth simultaneously (one high, the other low).

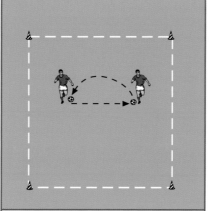

OBJECTIVES
• See Exercise 1

VARIATIONS

1. Goalkeepers bounce the balls instead of throwing them.
2. Goalkeepers face each other and run sideways; at the coach's signal they throw their balls to each other (one-handed).

EXERCISE 4

Setup is as above.
One goalkeeper runs after the other. At the coach's signal, GK1 stops and crouches, legs slightly apart. GK2 rolls the ball between them, vaults over and falls on the ball (alternating between diving to the left and to the right). Afterwards, players switch roles.

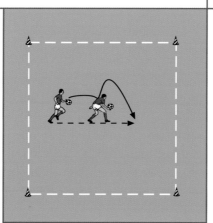

OBJECTIVES
• See Exercise 1

VARIATION

GK2 dives for the ball instead of falling on it.

Coordination Exercises with Coach and Ball

EXERCISE 1

Two goalkeepers practice with the coach (C), who has a ball.
Goalkeepers run side by side, two yards apart; C runs beside them, three yards away. C throws a high ball to the far goalkeeper, who catches it. The other goalkeeper immediately runs sideways to the outside position. The receiver throws the ball back to C and switches to the inside position. Make sure players jump with the left leg on balls from the left (and vice versa).

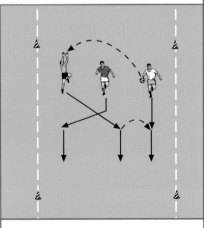

OBJECTIVES
- general warm-up
- motivational warm-up
- coordination training
- goalkeeper-specific technique training

VARIATIONS
1. At C's signal, the outside goalkeeper turns around once completely, then catches the ball.
2. The outside goalkeeper runs through the gap between C and the other goalkeeper and catches the ball.
3. After catching the ball, the outside goalkeeper switches to C's other side and catches another ball from the other side.

EXERCISE 2

Setup is as above.
The coach (C) runs between the two goalkeepers and throws the ball up to the left. The right goalkeeper runs in front of C and catches it while the left goalkeeper runs behind C to the right side. Make sure players jump with the correct leg. After running a certain distance, C starts throwing the ball up to the right, and players run in the opposite directions.

OBJECTIVES
- See exercise 1

VARIATIONS
1. Players must also do a coordination exercise.
2. Players do not switch sides. Instead, the receiver runs sideways to touch C, runs away sideways and catches a high ball from the side. Goalkeepers switch sides after running a certain distance.
3. At C's signal, both goalkeepers do forward rolls; then the basic exercise starts.

EXERCISE 3

Setup is as above.
One goalkeeper runs after the other while the coach (C, with a ball) runs beside them. At C's signal, the rear goalkeeper runs past the front one and catches a high ball from C.

OBJECTIVES
• See Exercise 1

VARIATIONS

1. The rear goalkeeper turns around once completely, then passes the front goalkeeper.
2. At C's signal, the rear goalkeeper stops. The front one quickly turns around, tags the rear one, turns around again and catches a high ball from C. Goalkeepers switch roles after running a certain distance.
3. The front goalkeeper does a forward roll before catching the ball.

EXERCISE 4

Setup is as above.
One goalkeeper runs after the other. At the coach's (C's) signal, the front goalkeeper stops with legs apart. The rear one crawls between them and stops in a crouching position. C throws a low ball to the standing goalkeeper, who jumps over the crouching one to catch it. Goalkeepers switch roles after running a certain distance.

OBJECTIVES
• See Exercise 1

VARIATION

At C's signal, the rear goalkeeper stops with legs apart. The front goalkeeper quickly runs around the rear one, crawls under and stops a ground ball (or catches a high ball) from C.

Practice Games and Exercises

EXERCISE 1

Three goalkeepers (GK1–3) practice together; if necessary, the coach (C) can be GK3. GK1 stands between two cones (two yards apart). GK2 and GK3 stand at two more cones placed five yards in front of GK1, to the right and left; each of them has a ball. GK2 drop-kicks the ball to GK1, who catches it and throws it back, then runs sideways to the other cone and catches a drop-kick from GK3, throws it back, runs sideways back to the first cone and starts over again.

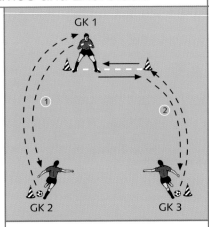

OBJECTIVES

- general warm-up
- motivational warm-up
- coordination training
- general and goalkeeper-specific technique training

VARIATIONS

1. GK1 turns around once completely while running from cone to cone.
2. GK1 places his hands on his back while turning (balance training).
3. GK2 and GK3 pass on the ground. GK1 dives to the right (or left) and rolls the ball back while still lying on the ground.
4. GK1 passes directly back on the ground with the right (or left) foot.
5. GK1 turns around once completely before passing back.

EXERCISE 2

Four goalkeepers (GK1–4) practice together; if necessary, the coach (C) can be GK4. Three cones (A, B and C) sit in a row, spaced seven yards apart. Cone D sits seven yards to the right of Cone B. Each goalkeeper stands at a cone.

GK1, GK4 and GK3 drop-kick balls to GK2 (in that order: 1-2, 4-2, 3-2, 4-2, 1-2 etc.). GK2 catches the balls and throws them back. After each catch, GK2 quickly puts his hands behind his back, then in front again. Goalkeepers switch roles after 10 rounds.

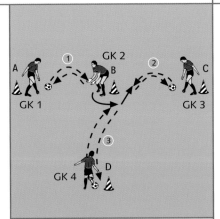

OBJECTIVES

- See Exercise 1

VARIATIONS

1. GK2 drop-kicks the balls back.
2. Before catching each ball, GK2 turns around once completely.

EXERCISE 3

Setup is as above. The goal-keeper at Cone D (GK4) has several balls and is the designated thrower or passer (players switch roles after several rounds).
GK4 throws a high ball to Cone B, and GK3 runs to catch it there (takeoff leg: left). At the same time, GK2 runs to Cone C. GK3 catches the ball and throws it back to GK4, who throws a high ball to Cone B. This time GK1 runs to catch it there (takeoff leg: right) while GK3 runs to Cone A, etc.

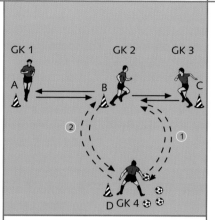

VARIATIONS

1. Players do forward rolls before switching cones or catching the ball.
2. Instead of catching the ball, players punch it back with both fists.
3. Players do different coordination exercises (e.g. turn around before running to the ball, forward roll before switching cones).

OBJECTIVES

• See Exercise 1

EXERCISE 4

Setup is as above.
GK4 passes on the ground to Cone B, and GK3 runs there and passes the ball back directly with the right foot, then switches to Cone A. GK1 runs to Cone B, passes the ball directly back to GK4 with the left foot and switches to Cone C, etc.

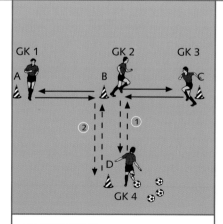

VARIATIONS

1. Players do coordination exercises before passing back.
2. GK3 receives and controls the ball with the right foot, dribbles around Cone B and passes back to GK4 with the left, then switches to Cone A, etc.

OBJECTIVES

• See Exercise 1

Teaching Technical Skills

Introduction

In the following pages we present practical, goalkeeper-specific technique exercises suitable for youth players. For each technique there are three basic exercise types, which can be changed and combined with one another. The levels of intensity and difficulty depend on players' ability level.

Exercise Type 1: combined technique and coordination training

Exercise Type 2: multiple player technique training

Exercise Type 3: exercises on the goal

Here are a few additional suggestions:

Coordination

As always, coordination training for 12- to 14-year-olds should never be separate; instead, it should take place during warm-up and in combination with technique exercises.

Tactics

Certain tactics – positional play, set plays, 1 v. 1 against a solo forward and winning the ball – are addressed in the third basic exercise. However, the bulk of tactics training should take place during regular sessions with the full team. Some tactics, such as organizing the defense with brief commands, can only be practiced in practice games and exercises focusing on group or team tactics. During these exercises, your job is to watch your goalkeepers and guide them in coaching their teammates. Of course, the teammates have to be involved as well (agree on commands and hand signals).

Condition

12- to 14-year-old goalkeepers should concentrate on the following aspects of condition:

1. speed training (in the context of coordination training)
2. soccer-specific and general stretching exercises (mobility training)
3. general strengthening
4. endurance training (through jogging or by using the goalkeeper as a field player during the cool-down game).

Character Development

You also need to think about motivation; players' willingness to get involved and their attitude toward practice and match play should be improved.

One-on-one discussions are a good way for you to reinforce players' character development.

Organization

On all exercises on the goal (Exercise Type 3), we recommend placing an extra cone in the center of the goal, for better orientation and to teach positional play. The goalkeeper should stay on an imaginary line between the center of the goal (the cone) and the ball.

High Balls: Catching Shots from the Front and Side

In the following pages, please note that we have intentionally omitted exercises specifically for practicing the basic position and catching low balls from the front and side. For these techniques, please turn to the corresponding sections of the previous chapter.

You can also turn to the previous chapter for more on our first technique, catching high balls from the front and side.

Stay alert and engaged, even under pressure.

Technique and Coordination

BASIC EXERCISE 1A

The goalkeeper stands at a cone five yards behind a hurdle (or similar object), which has another cone beyond it. The coach (C) has several balls and stands five yards to one side of the hurdle. The goalkeeper catches a high ball from C, jumps over the hurdle, touches the cone, jumps back over the hurdle and rolls the ball to a target goal. C's throws should be timed so that the goalkeeper has to catch balls from both right and left.

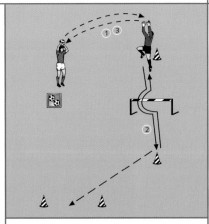

FOCUS ON

- quick reaction times
- one-legged takeoff with the leg closer to the ball, fully extending the ankle, knee and hip of the takeoff leg
- catching balls from both sides

VARIATIONS

1. The goalkeeper crawls under the hurdle.
2. The rear cone is placed a bit to one side, so that the goalkeeper can do a forward roll after the first jump over the hurdle. After touching the far cone, the goalkeeper does another forward roll toward the hurdle, crawls under it and catches the next ball.

BASIC EXERCISE 1B

The goalkeeper stands in the center of a five-yard-wide goal. In front of the goal is a row of four cones, spaced one yard apart. The coach (C) has a ball and stands beside the cones, five yards away. The goalkeeper slaloms through the cones at an easy pace, runs backwards beside them back to the goal and then catches a high ball from C (while moving forward again).

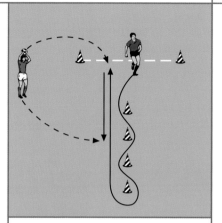

FOCUS ON
- See Exercise 1A

VARIATION
On the way back, the goalkeeper slaloms backwards through the cones.

Multiple Player Technique Training

BASIC EXERCISE 2A

Three or four goalkeepers (each one has a ball) and the coach (C) move around inside a 10 x 10-yard field. Goalkeepers bounce their balls while running. C calls a name, and that player throws a ball to C, does a forward roll and catches a high ball from C.

FOCUS ON:
- quick reaction times
- jumping to catch the ball at the highest point possible
- taking off with one leg and swinging the other knee up

VARIATIONS
1. Goalkeepers do forward rolls before catching the ball.
2. One goalkeeper gives C a ball, then runs in amongst the other players. C calls a name, and that player throws a ball to the goalkeeper who does not have one. These two run to meet each other and bump each other with their shoulders. Then the goalkeeper who threw the ball catches a high ball from C and throws it back, and the exercise starts over again.

BASIC EXERCISE 2B

Three cones mark out a triangle (five yards on a side). A goalkeeper stands at each cone (GK1 at Cone A, GK2 at B and GK3 at C); GK2 has a ball. GK2 throws a high ball to GK1, who runs all the way around Cone A before jumping to catch it. Then GK1 throws to GK3, who runs around Cone C before catching, etc.

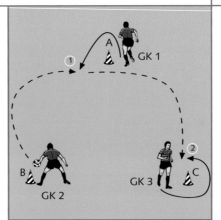

FOCUS ON
• See Exercise 2A

VARIATIONS
1. GK2 throws the ball to GK1, then does a forward roll and runs backwards back to Cone B.
2. GK2 kicks a high ball to GK1, etc.
3. At the coach's signal, players start throwing in the opposite direction.

Exercises on the Goal

BASIC EXERCISE 3A

GK1 stands in the center of a standard goal. GK2 and GK3 stand 16 yards in front of the goal, to the left and right; each one has a ball. The coach (C) has a ball and stands five yards to one side of the goal. At C's signal, GK1 runs forward to the post, touches it and runs sideways back to the center of the goal. Then C throws a high ball in front of the goal. GK1 catches it and rolls it back to C. C calls a number ("2" or "3"), and that player tries to score with a drop-kick.

FOCUS ON
• powerful takeoff from the ground, swinging the other knee and both arms up
• on the drop-kick, stretching both arms out in front and dropping the ball, or throwing it up with one hand

VARIATIONS
1. After touching the post, GK1 does a backwards roll.
2. GK1 must do a forward roll toward the designated attacker before blocking the shot.
3. GK1 catches C's ball and rolls it to GK2; GK3 tries to score with a drop-kick.

BASIC EXERCISE 3B

GK1 stands in a standard goal, GK2 on the goal box line, and GK3 at a cone about 18 yards in front of the center of the goal. The coach (C) has a ball and stands to the left or right, outside the penalty box. C kicks a high ball to the edge of the goal box, and GK1 tries to catch it in spite of GK2's interference. Then GK1 rolls it to GK3, who dribbles to the goal and plays 1 v. 1 against GK1 to score.

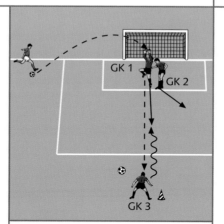

VARIATION

While GK3 plays 1 v. 1 to score, GK2 runs to the penalty box line. After the 1 v. 1 play, C kicks another high ball in front of the goal, and GK2 tries to score with a header or volley. GK1 tries either to catch the ball first (ideally), or to block the shot. Players switch roles and positions after several rounds.

FOCUS ON

- taking a "low" position (without squatting too low)
- standing loosely and shifting the weight forward by bending at the knees and hips

BASIC EXERCISE 3C

GK1 stands in a standard goal, GK2 five yards in front of the right post, and the coach five yards in front of the left one. GK2 has a ball and throws it up and forward about three yards. GK1 catches it and rolls it back, then runs and dives for a ground ball from C aimed at the left corner of the goal.
Players switch roles and positions after several rounds (practice on both sides!).

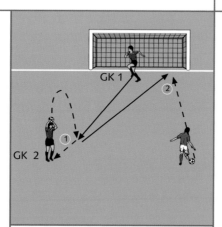

VARIATIONS

1. GK1 does a backwards roll before catching GK2's ball.
2. GK1 does a forward roll before diving for C's ground ball.
3. Instead of shooting at the corner, C throws the ball up and forward, and GK2 kicks a second ball at the right corner.
4. GK1 always has to turn around before catching or diving for the ball.

FOCUS ON

- taking a long stride toward the ball on the last step
- taking off with the leg closer to the ball (the right leg on balls from the right and vice versa)

Diving and Rolling Sideways on Ground Balls

When diving and rolling, always keep your eyes on the ball!

Technique and Coordination

BASIC EXERCISE 1A

The goalkeeper stands at a cone one yard behind a hurdle (or similar object). A row of four cones leads toward the outside leg of the hurdle. The coach (C) has a ball and stands seven yards away from the cones. At C's signal, the goalkeeper jumps sideways (with both legs) over the hurdle, runs sideways and dives in front of the cones to keep C's ball from hitting them.

FOCUS ON
- rolling over the hips, side and shoulder
- "stopping the ball out in front": on a ball to the left, taking a short step toward it with the left foot and stopping it as soon as possible

VARIATIONS

1. The goalkeeper crawls under the hurdle.
2. The goalkeeper stands to the left of the hurdle and does a double jump.
3. The goalkeeper hops in place, then quickly jumps over the hurdle to the ball at C's signal.

BASIC EXERCISE 1B

The goalkeeper stands at a cone. Three yards in front of the cone are three five-yard-wide goals (A, B, C), staggered and placed at different distances. The coach (C) has a ball and stands five yards behind the center goal. At C's signal ("A," "B" or "C"), the goalkeeper runs at top speed to the goal indicated and dives (sideways at Goals A and B, forward at Goal C) for a ground ball from C.

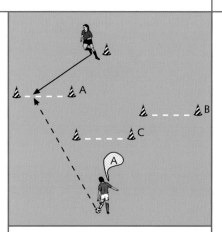

FOCUS ON
• See Exercise 1A

VARIATIONS
1. Instead of calling out names, C uses hand signals.
2. The goalkeeper does a forward roll before running to the ball.
3. The goalkeeper starts from various starting positions.

BASIC EXERCISE 1C

The goalkeeper stands in a six-yard-wide goal. In front of the goal are two cones spaced three yards apart. The coach (C) has a ball and stands three yards beyond the second cone. The goalkeeper runs sideways (from right to left) between the cones and toward C. C passes on the ground to the goalkeeper, who passes back with the inside of the right foot, then runs backwards alongside the cones back to the goal. As soon as the goalkeeper runs past the cone closer to the goal, C kicks a ground ball at the right corner, and the goalkeeper dives for it.

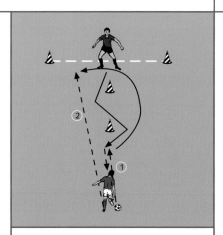

FOCUS ON
• See Exercise 1A

VARIATIONS
1. After running sideways, the goalkeeper does a forward roll and passes C's ground ball back with the inside of the right foot.
2. After the back pass, the goalkeeper does a backwards roll toward the goal.

Multiple Player Technique Training

BASIC EXERCISE 2A

GK1 stands in the center of a six-yard-wide goal. C stands three yards behind GK1, and GK2 has a ball and stands three yards to C's right. C throws a ball at GK1's left shoulder; GK1 turns around quickly and catches it before it hits the ground. Then GK1 throws it back to C and dives toward the left corner for a ground ball from GK2.

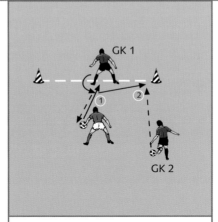

FOCUS ON

- keeping your eyes on the ball
- bringing your leg forward: on a dive to the left, the right knee should come slightly forward (and vice versa) to keep you from rolling over backwards

BASIC EXERCISE 2B

GK1 starts out in push-up position in the center of a six-yard-wide goal. GK2 has a ball and stands behind the goal; C stands five yards in front of it. GK3 has a ball and stands three yards to the left of C.

At C's signal, GK2 passes under GK1 to C. GK1 stands up quickly, turns around to the left and dives to the right for a ground ball from GK3. Then GK1 rolls over, rolls the ball back while still lying on the ground and dives to the other side for a ground ball from C.

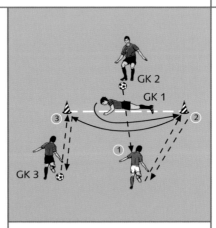

FOCUS ON

- See Exercise 2A

VARIATIONS

GK1 starts out lying face-down; C has a ball, but GK2 does not. At C's signal, GK2 jumps over GK1. C passes on the ground to the left of GK2, who dives for the ball. As soon as GK2 jumps over, GK1 quickly stands up and dives to the right for a ground ball from GK3. Then GK1 and GK2 switch positions, and the exercise starts over again. GK3 and GK1 switch roles and positions after two rounds.

Exercises on the Goal

BASIC EXERCISE 3A

GK1 stands in a standard goal, next to the right post. C stands in front of the goal, GK2 at or near the left penalty box corner; each one has a ball. C kicks a ground ball in front of the goal. GK1 falls to the left for it, rolls it back to C while still lying on the ground and gets up quickly. At the same moment, GK2 kicks a ground ball, and GK1 passes it back with the inside of the left foot. Then GK1 turns to the right and runs toward C, who kicks another ground ball at the right corner of the goal; GK1 dives for it.

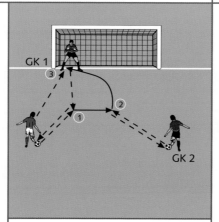

VARIATIONS

1. GK2 throws a low ball to GK1, who volleys it back with the left foot.
2. GK2 throws a high ball to one side of GK1, who catches it and throws it back.
3. First C throws a high ball in front of the goal. GK1 catches it and throws it back to C. GK2 kicks a ground ball to GK1's left, and C kicks a second ground ball to the right.

FOCUS ON
- reaching for the ball with both hands
- getting one hand behind the ball and the other on (or behind) it
- general technical skills (passing)

BASIC EXERCISE 3B

Set up a four-yard-wide goal on the penalty box line in front of a standard goal. The goalkeeper stands at the right post; C has a ball and stands five yards in front of the center of the goal. C kicks a ground ball to the left of the goalkeeper, who dives to the left for it, throws it back to C while still lying on the ground, gets up quickly and runs around the left cone and back to the big goal. Then C throws a high ball at the right corner of the big goal.

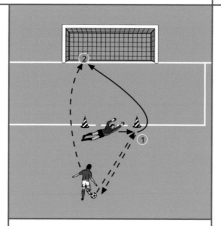

VARIATIONS

1. The goalkeeper starts out in push-up position, or lying face-up or face-down.
2. After running around the left cone, the goalkeeper does a forward roll before running to the big goal.

FOCUS ON
- reaching for the ball with both hands
- getting one hand behind the ball and the other on (or behind) it
- securing the ball against the body

When you jump, extend the jumping leg and pull the other leg up.

Balls in the Air: Diving, Jumping and Rolling

Technique and Coordination

BASIC EXERCISE 1A

The goalkeeper starts out in push-up position in the center of a six-yard-wide goal. To the goalkeeper's left is a row of several cones. The coach (C) has a ball and stands three yards in front of the goal. At C's signal, the goalkeeper rolls over the right shoulder, gets up quickly and jumps over the cones for a throw from C.

FOCUS ON
- taking one or more steps to the side ("step – step – jump"), taking a longer stride on the last step and moving diagonally forward
- diving straight toward the ball

VARIATIONS
1. After getting up, the goal-keeper runs around the right post, does a forward roll, then jumps for C's ball.
2. After getting up, the goal-keeper passes a ground ball back to C with the inside of the right foot, touches the right post, then jumps for a throw from C.
3. The goalkeeper jumps directly from the push-up position over the cones, rolls over the left shoulder, gets up quickly and jumps back over the cones for a throw from C.

BASIC EXERCISE 1B

The goalkeeper stands at one end of a three-yard-wide lane formed by two rows of cones. The coach (C) has a ball and stands at the other end (two yards away) facing the goalkeeper. At C's signal ("left" or "right"), the goalkeeper does a forward roll and jumps left or right over the cones for a throw from C.

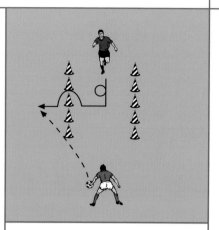

VARIATION

The goalkeeper stands facing away from C. At C's signal ("left" or "right"), the goalkeeper does a backwards roll and quickly turns to face C before jumping over the designated row of cones for the ball.

FOCUS ON
• taking one or more steps to the side ("step – step – jump"), taking a longer stride on the last step and moving diagonally forward

Multiple Player Technique Training

BASIC EXERCISE 2A

GK1 stands in the center of a six-yard-wide goal, with GK2 to the right in push-up position. C has a ball and stands three yards in front of GK1. At C's signal, GK1 jumps over GK2 and back again for a throw from C (taking off fast and explosively with both legs).

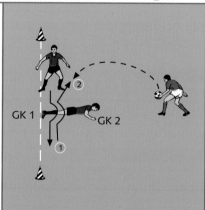

VARIATIONS
1. GK1 does a diving roll over GK2, touches the far post and jumps back over GK2 for a throw from C.
2. GK1 jumps (with both legs) over GK2 and immediately goes into push-up position. Then GK2 quickly gets up, dives to the left for a ground ball from C, throws it back while still lying on the ground, gets up again and jumps over GK1 for a throw from C. Afterwards players switch roles and positions.

FOCUS ON
• bending, then straightening the takeoff leg; swinging the arms and the other knee up
• shifting the center of gravity over the takeoff leg

BASIC EXERCISE 2B

Two goalkeepers (GK1 and GK2) practice with the coach (C). Two small hurdles stand in front of GK1. On each side of the second hurdle is a perpendicular row of cones. C stands at the end of the right row, GK2 at the end of the left (each one has a ball). At C's signal ("left" or "right"), GK1 does two two-legged jumps over the hurdles (no extra jump between them) and dives over the designated row of cones for a throw from C or GK2. Then GK1 returns to the starting position, and the exercise starts over again.

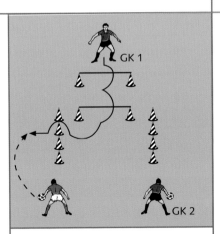

FOCUS ON
• See Exercise 2A

VARIATIONS

1. GK1 jumps sideways (still two-legged jumps) over the hurdles.
2. The second hurdle is taller than the first. GK1 does a two-legged jump over the first one, crawls under the second and dives for the ball.

Exercises on the Goal

BASIC EXERCISE 3A

Two goalkeepers (GK1 and GK2) practice with the coach (C). GK1 stands in a standard goal. Six yards in front of the goal are five cones. C stands two yards to the right of the cones; GK2 has a ball and stands 15 yards in front of the goal. C throws a high ball at the goal; GK1 punches it back to C with both fists, jumps over the cones and passes a ground ball back to GK2 with the inside of the left foot. Then GK1 turns to C and dives back over the cones for C's throw.

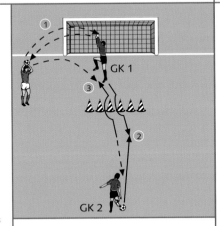

FOCUS ON
• practicing on both sides
• explosive takeoff with the takeoff leg (brief contact with the ground)
• accelerating directly toward the ball
• a short jump straight for the ball

VARIATIONS

1. GK1 does a forward roll before passing the ground ball back to GK2.
2. After passing back to GK2, GK1 jumps back over the cones, does a forward roll toward the goal, turns toward C and dives over the cones again for C's throw.

BASIC EXERCISE 3B

Setup is as above, except GK1 starts out to the left of the cones, facing the coach (C). GK1 runs forward and receives a ground ball from C, passes it back with the inside of the right foot, runs backwards past the cones on the other side, then runs forward again and passes another ground ball back to C with the inside of the left foot. Then GK1 does a forward roll toward GK2, heads a high ball back into GK2's arms, turns back toward C and dives over the cones for C's throw.

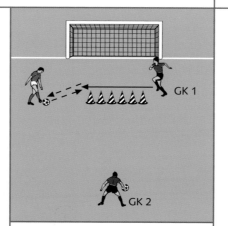

FOCUS ON

- practicing accurate passing
- explosive takeoff with the takeoff leg (brief contact with the ground)
- accelerating directly toward the ball
- a short jump straight for the ball

BASIC EXERCISE 3C

Setup is as above.
GK1 starts by jumping over the cones for a low (or high) ball thrown by the coach (C). After GK1 throws it back, GK2 throws a high ball at the goal. GK1 jumps over the cones toward the goal and tries to catch the ball or deflect it to the side, either beside or over the goal.

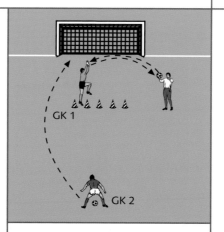

FOCUS ON

- explosive takeoff with the takeoff leg (brief contact with the ground)
- accelerating directly toward the ball
- a short jump straight for the ball

Deflection Techniques

NOTE:

You can also use some of the exercises in the section "Diving and Rolling Sideways on Ground Balls" for practicing deflection techniques.

Technique and Coordination

BASIC EXERCISE 1A

The goalkeeper starts out in push-up position in the center of a five-yard-wide goal, head toward the right post. The coach (C) has a ball and stands five yards in front of the goal. At C's signal, the goalkeeper gets up quickly and turns to the left, toward C, who kicks a ground ball toward the other post. The goalkeeper tries to deflect the ball to the side with the heel of the left hand.

FOCUS ON
- deflecting with the heel of the hand
- keeping the wrist firm
- thrusting forward from the elbow to hit the ball

VARIATIONS

1. At C's signal, the goalkeeper gets up quickly, does a backwards roll and runs forward and to the right for a ground ball from C, deflecting it to the side with the heel of the right hand.
2. The goalkeeper does a forward roll directly from the push-up position, runs around the left post and then runs sideways to deflect a ground ball from C toward the left post with the ball of the left hand.

BASIC EXERCISE 1B

The goalkeeper lies face-down in the center of a small goal, head toward the coach (C), who has several balls and stands six or seven yards in front of the goal. At C's signal, the goalkeeper gets up quickly and moves left to deflect a ground ball from C to the side with the heel of the left hand. Then the goal-keeper rolls over the buttocks, gets up quickly and moves right to deflect a second ground ball from C to the side with the heel of the right hand.

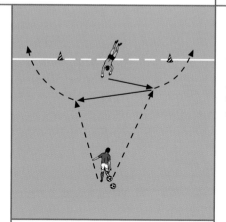

VARIATION

The goalkeeper lies face-down as above, but with the feet toward C.
Sequence is the same; C calls out "left" or "right" and kicks the first ground ball to that side.

FOCUS ON
• See Exercise 1A

Multiple Player Technique Training

BASIC EXERCISE 2A

Two goalkeepers practice with the coach (C). GK1 starts out in push-up position in the center of a six-yard-wide goal. GK2 and C stand on opposite sides of the goal, each four yards away (each has a ball). C kicks a ground ball to the right of GK1, who dives directly from the push-up position for the ball and deflects it to the side with the heel of the right hand. Then GK1 quickly gets up, turns to the right and dives to the right for a ground ball from GK2.

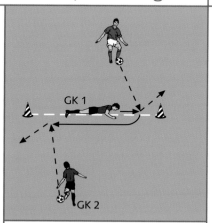

FOCUS ON
• deflecting the ball as soon as possible
• deflecting the ball to the side

BASIC EXERCISE 2B

GK1 stands in the center of a six-yard-wide goal, GK2 two yards away from the right post. The coach (C) has two balls and stands six or seven yards in front of the goal. C throws a low (or high) ball to the right of GK1, who deflects it to GK2 with the heel of the right hand (thrusting from the elbow). Then C kicks a ground ball to the left of GK1, who falls and deflects it to the side with the heel of the left hand.

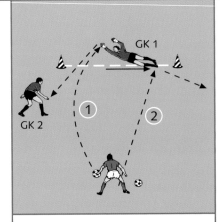

FOCUS ON

- deflecting the ball as soon as possible
- deflecting the ball to the side
- practicing on both sides

Exercises on the Goal

BASIC EXERCISE 3A

The goalkeeper stands in the center of a standard goal with a cone five yards in front of it. The coach (C) has a ball and stands in front of the goal on the right, four yards away. At C's signal, the goalkeeper does a forward roll toward the cone, runs around it and runs back toward the goal. Then the goalkeeper moves right to deflect a ground ball from C to the side with the heel of the right hand. After several rounds, C switches to the left side of the goal, and the exercise starts over again.

FOCUS ON

- deflecting with the heel of the hand
- keeping the wrist firm
- thrusting forward from the elbow to hit the ball
- deflecting the ball as soon as possible

VARIATIONS

1. C starts with a ground ball at the goalkeeper, who passes it back with the inside of the right foot; then the exercise proceeds as above.
2. C starts with a ground ball to the left of the goalkeeper, who dives for it, rolls it back to C while still lying on the ground, gets up quickly and runs around the cone.

BASIC EXERCISE 3B

GK1 stands in the center of a standard goal, GK2 four yards away from the right post. The coach (C) has a ball and stands four yards away from the left post.

First GK1 punches a ball back to GK2 with both fists, then does a backwards roll toward the goal, gets up quickly, turns toward C and deflects a ground ball to the side with the heel of the left hand.

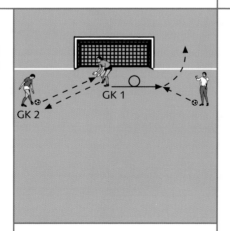

FOCUS ON
• See Exercise 3A

BASIC EXERCISE 3C

Place five cones in a row in front of a standard goal. The goalkeeper starts out in push-up position; the coach has two balls and stands two yards behind the far cone. At C's signal, the goalkeeper stands up, runs forward to the far cone, then around it and backwards toward the goal on the other side. As soon as the goalkeeper runs past the cone nearest the goal, C shoots on the ground at the goal's left corner. The goalkeeper dives, deflects the ball to the side with the heel of the left hand, gets up quickly and jumps over the cones for a throw from C.

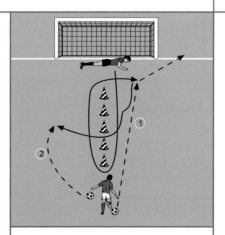

FOCUS ON
• See Exercise 3A

Throwing, Kicking, Punting, Drop-Kicking

On throws, take a step to brace yourself, draw the ball back and extend your other arm forward.

Technique and Coordination

BASIC EXERCISE 1A

The goalkeeper stands facing a hurdle; the coach (C) has a ball and stands beside it, 15 yards away. The goalkeeper jumps (one-legged) over the hurdle, catches a low drop-kick from C in front of the body, drop-kicks it back and runs backwards around the hurdle. Then C drop-kicks the ball at the goalkeeper, who catches it, throws it back to C, and jumps over the hurdle (one-legged) again; the exercise starts over again. After several rounds, the goalkeeper switches sides and takes off with the other leg on the jumps.

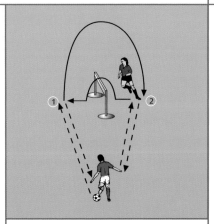

FOCUS ON (DROP-KICK)
- stretching both arms out in front and dropping the ball, or throwing it up with one hand
- raising the knee of the kicking leg (the foot meets the ball below knee level)

VARIATIONS

1. After catching C's first drop-kick, the goalkeeper runs backwards around the hurdle with the ball, then throws it back to C and jumps over the hurdle again; the exercise starts over again.
2. Sequence is as above, except the goalkeeper crawls under the hurdle.

BASIC EXERCISE 1B

The goalkeeper stands right next to a hurdle, the coach (C) 15 yards away. Using the right foot, the goalkeeper kicks a ball lying to the right of the hurdle to C, who catches it. Then the goalkeeper jumps over the hurdle and catches a high ball from C, places it to the left of the hurdle and kicks it to C with the left foot. Then the goalkeeper jumps over the hurdle again and catches the next high ball from C.

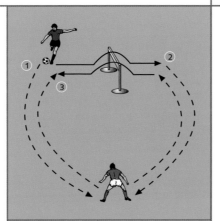

VARIATION

The goalkeeper drop-kicks or punts (or volleys) the ball to C.

FOCUS ON (KICKING)

- keeping the standing leg behind or next to the ball
- approaching the ball diagonally
- hitting the ball squarely in the middle

Multiple Player Technique Training

BASIC EXERCISE 2A

Two goalkeepers (GK1 and GK2) practice with the coach (C). GK1 stands in front of one cone and between two others (each two yards away). C and GK2 stand eight yards in front of GK1, C on the left, GK2 on the right; each one has a ball. GK1 runs sideways to the left cone, catches a low ball from C there and drop-kicks it back. Then GK1 runs sideways around the rear cone to the right one and catches a low drop-kick from GK2. GK1 throws it back to GK2 and runs sideways to the left cone again, following the same path.

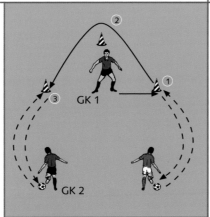

VARIATIONS

1. C and GK2 stand 15 yards away from GK1 and kick high balls instead of low ones; otherwise the sequence remains the same.
2. GK1 punts (or volleys) the balls back to C and GK2.
3. Take away one ball. GK1 catches C's ball and drop-kicks or throws it diagonally to GK2.

FOCUS ON

- keeping the ankle firm and the toes pointing downward
- pointing the toes of the standing foot in the direction of the kick
- placing the standing leg even with the ball

BASIC EXERCISE 2B

Three goalkeepers practice together. GK2 stands in a five-yard-wide goal. GK1 stands 15 yards in front of GK2, GK3 15 yards behind; each of them has a ball. GK1 drop-kicks precisely to GK2, who catches it in front of the body and drop-kicks it back to GK1. Then GK2 turns around and receives a drop-kick from GK3, etc.

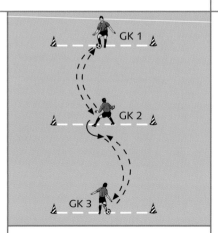

FOCUS ON
• See Exercise 2A

VARIATIONS

1. GK1 punts (or volleys) a high ball to GK2, who catches it and throws it back, then turns to receive a punt (or volley) from GK3, etc.
2. Take away one ball. GK1 passes precisely to GK2, who catches it, turns around and throws it to GK3. GK3 catches it and drop-kicks it to GK1, who kicks it to GK2 again, etc.

Exercises on the Goal

BASIC EXERCISE 3A

Two goalkeepers each stand in a five-yard-wide goal (25 yards apart) with a standard goal halfway between them.
The goalkeepers punt (or volley) or drop-kick a ball back and forth over the big goal.

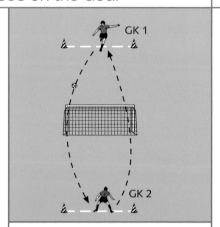

FOCUS ON (PUNTING)
• taking a few steps and then throwing the ball up a short distance with both hands
• holding the ball out in front of the body with both arms extended

VARIATION

GK1 kicks a high ball over the big goal to GK2, who receives it like a back pass and stops it. Then GK2 kicks a high ball over the goal to GK1, etc.

BASIC EXERCISE 3B

Setup is as above.
GK1 throws the ball over the big goal to GK2, who receives and stops it like a back pass. Then GK2 kicks the ball over the goal to GK1, who catches it and throws it back over to GK2, etc. Players switch roles after several rounds.

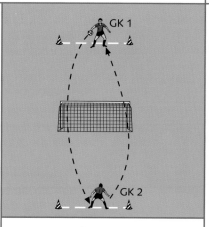

FOCUS ON (KICKING)

- approaching the ball diagonally
- hitting the ball squarely in the middle
- letting the kicking leg swing through the kick

BASIC EXERCISE 3C

GK1 and GK2 each stand in a standard goal (25 yards apart). GK3 has a ball and stands next to GK1's goal. GK3 kicks the ball to GK2, who catches it and tries to score against GK1 with a well-aimed drop-kick. Then the exercise starts over again. Goalkeepers rotate clockwise if one of them scores, or after several rounds.

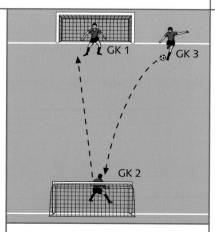

FOCUS ON

- See Exercise 3B

VARIATIONS

1. GK3 drop-kicks the ball to GK2, who receives it like a back pass and tries to score against GK1 with an instep kick.
2. GK3 punts (or volleys) the ball to GK2, who catches it and tries to score against GK1 with a punt (or volley).
3. Move the two goals closer together. GK3 drop-kicks the ball to GK2, who catches it and tries to score against GK1 with a throw.

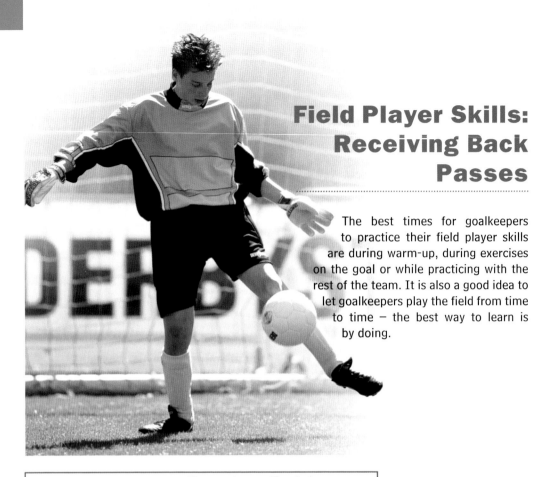

Field Player Skills: Receiving Back Passes

The best times for goalkeepers to practice their field player skills are during warm-up, during exercises on the goal or while practicing with the rest of the team. It is also a good idea to let goalkeepers play the field from time to time — the best way to learn is by doing.

Multiple Player Technique Training

BASIC EXERCISE 1

Three cones form a triangle (seven yards on each side). A goalkeeper stands at each cone. GK1 and GK2 each have a ball and take turns kicking well-aimed ground balls to GK3. GK3 passes GK1's ball back directly with the inside of the left foot, steps sideways toward GK2 and passes GK2's ball back with the inside of the right foot. Then GK3 steps sideways and turns to face GK1, etc.

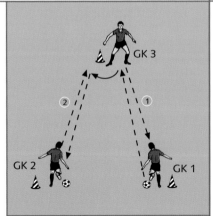

FOCUS ON
- general technique training
- practicing with both feet

VARIATIONS

1. GK3 passes GK1's ball back with the inside of the right foot and GK2's with the left.
2. Take away one ball. GK1 kicks a well-aimed ground ball to GK3, who passes it directly to GK2 with the inside of the right foot. GK2 kicks a well-aimed ground ball back to GK3, who passes it directly to GK1 with the inside of the left foot, etc.

Note: On this exercise in particular, pay attention to the goalkeepers' positions in relation to the ball; they should be turning ahead of time to face it.

BASIC EXERCISE 2

Five cones (all spaced seven yards apart and numbered from one through five) form an "X" pattern. Three goalkeepers and the coach (C) stand at the outside cones; each one has a ball. A fourth goalkeeper stands at the center cone without a ball. The exercise begins with a pass on the ground from C to the goalkeeper in the center. This player passes back directly with the inside of the right foot, then turns to the left to face the first goalkeeper, passes that player's ball back directly with the inside of the right foot, then turns to the left to face the next goalkeeper, etc.

NOTE
- for the center goalkeeper: passing accurately to the outside players; stepping sideways to the left or right and assuming the optimal position in relation to the ball as quickly as possible

VARIATIONS

1. The center goalkeeper passes four times with the right foot. Then C kicks a ground ball to the left, and the center goalkeeper passes directly back with the inside of the left foot, turns to the right and passes the next player's ball directly back with the left foot, etc. The center goalkeeper does two rounds with the right foot and two with the left; then players switch roles and positions.
2. Use different balls (including tennis or mini soccer balls).

Exercises on the Goal

BASIC EXERCISE 3

Three goalkeepers (GK1–3) practice with the coach (C). GK1 stands in a standard goal. C has several balls and stands 25 yards in front of GK1, with GK2 and GK3 each 25 yards away diagonally to the left and right. C passes on the ground to GK1, who receives the ball and passes on the ground with the inside instep to GK2. GK2 passes directly to C, who passes on the ground to GK1 again. GK1 receives the ball and passes with the inside instep to GK3. GK3 passes directly to C, and the exercise starts over again.

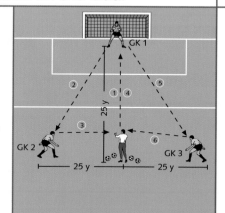

FOCUS ON
- passing accurately
- field player techniques in general (inside instep kick)

VARIATIONS

1. GK1 passes directly to GK2 and GK3.
2. C passes to GK1's left and right; GK1 has to decide which goalkeeper to pass back to. (Tip: Always direct the ball away from the goal.)
3. GK1 kicks high balls; GK2 and GK3 pass directly to the coach as above.

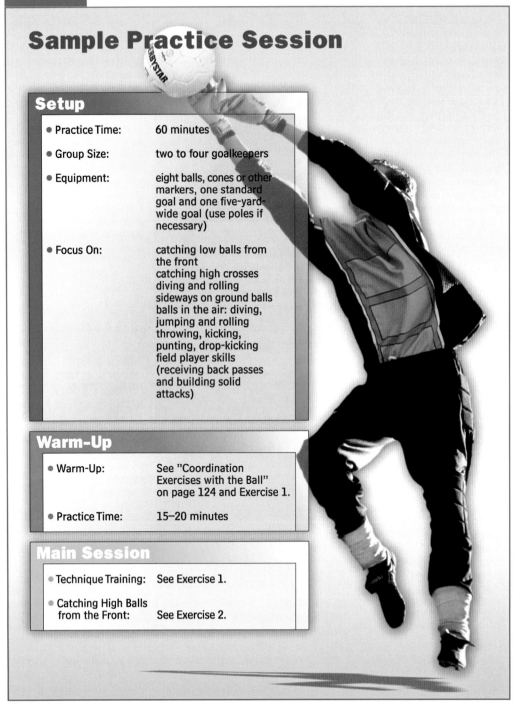

Illustr. 10

Sample Practice Session

Setup

- **Practice Time:** 60 minutes

- **Group Size:** two to four goalkeepers

- **Equipment:** eight balls, cones or other markers, one standard goal and one five-yard-wide goal (use poles if necessary)

- **Focus On:** catching low balls from the front
catching high crosses
diving and rolling sideways on ground balls
balls in the air: diving, jumping and rolling
throwing, kicking, punting, drop-kicking
field player skills (receiving back passes and building solid attacks)

Warm-Up

- **Warm-Up:** See "Coordination Exercises with the Ball" on page 124 and Exercise 1.

- **Practice Time:** 15–20 minutes

Main Session

- **Technique Training:** See Exercise 1.

- **Catching High Balls from the Front:** See Exercise 2.

Diving Sideways on Ground Balls

EXERCISE 1

GK1 squats on the ground next to GK2; the coach (C) has several balls and stands five yards in front of GK1. At C's signal, GK2 jumps over GK1, who immediately goes into push-up position. Then GK2 crawls under GK1 and dives to the side for a ground ball from C. Then GK2 squats and GK1 jumps. Note: C should not pass until the goalkeeper finishes crawling and stands up again.

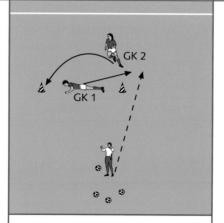

FOCUS ON
- rolling over the hips, side and shoulder
- "stopping the ball out in front": on a ground ball to the right, taking a short step toward it with the right foot (or vice versa) and stopping it as soon as possible

EXERCISE 2

Three yards in front of a goal-keeper (who has a ball) is a row of several cones. Immediately behind it is a six-yard-wide goal marked by two more cones. The coach (C) stands five yards in front of this goal. At C's signal, the goalkeeper drop-kicks the ball to C, immediately does a forward roll over the row of cones and dives to the side for a ground ball from C. Just before the goalkeeper jumps over the cones, C indicates which side the pass will be on.

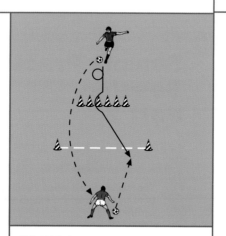

FOCUS ON
- drop-kick: stretching both arms out in front and dropping the ball, or throwing it up with one hand
- stopping ground balls: rolling over the hips, side and shoulder

Diving / Jumping and Rolling Sideways

EXERCISE

The goalkeeper starts out in push-up position; a cone sits three yards to the right. The coach (C) has a ball and stands three yards in front of the goalkeeper. Left of the goal is a row of cones. At C's signal, the goalkeeper lies face-down, quickly rolls over to the left, gets up, touches the cone on the right and dives over the cones for a ball thrown by C. Switch sides after several rounds.

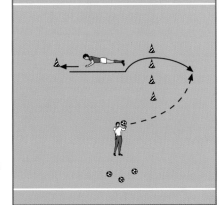

FOCUS ON

- shifting the center of gravity over the takeoff leg
- explosive takeoff with the takeoff leg (brief contact with the ground)
- accelerating directly toward the ball

Illustr. 11

Sample Practice Session, Part 2

Throwing, Kicking, Drop-Kicking

The following exercises focus on throwing, kicking, punting and drop-kicking, as well as field player techniques in general (safely receiving and controlling back passes and starting a solid attack). In addition, Exercise 2 trains players to receive crosses.

Practice time for both exercises is 15–20 minutes.

Motivational Exercises for 2–4 Goalkeepers

EXERCISE 1

GK1 stands in a standard goal; 20 yards away is a five-yard-wide goal placed at right angles to the first, approximately at the corner of the penalty box (GK2 stands here). Five yards in front of the smaller goal is a line, and a cone sits in the center of the penalty box line. The coach (C) has several balls and stands 15 yards in front of the smaller goal. C kicks a back pass to GK2, who receives it in front of the line, dribbles to the cone and shoots at GK1's goal. If GK1 scores, the goalkeepers switch roles.

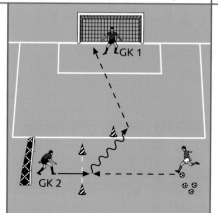

NOTE
• C should pass both on the ground and in the air (low and high).

VARIATION
C crosses in front of the smaller goal to GK2, who catches it in front of the line, runs to the cone and drop-kicks it at the big goal.

EXERCISE 2

GK1 stands in a standard goal, GK2 at a cone about 20 yards in front of it. The coach (C) has several balls and stands outside the penalty box. C crosses in front of the goal, and GK1 catches the cross and runs toward the cone. GK2 starts running toward the goal at the same time. GK1 runs around the cone and tries to score with a drop-kick (or throw); if successful, GK1 returns to the goal to start the next round. After several rounds, C starts crossing from the other side.

FOCUS ON (CROSSES)
• swinging the arms for momentum on the jump
• powerful takeoff from the ground, swinging the arms and the other leg up

NOTE
These two motivational exercises, combined, should last 15 to 20 minutes.

The Finishing Touches: Advanced Training with 14- to 18-Year-Olds

Concepts and Activities

Thanks to developmental and other age-specific factors, both 14- to 16-year-olds and 16- to 18-year-olds have essentially the same performance profile. At both age levels, goalkeepers have the same set of technical, tactical, conditional and psychological requirements to fulfill. Practice sessions differ only in duration and intensity. This level, starting at age 14, is what we call advanced training.

Notes on Training 14- to 18-Year-Olds

• The purpose of advanced training is to lay the groundwork for high-level performance. If a solid foundation already exists, it can be improved considerably through systematic training. Now is the time for players to optimize their tactical play and to adapt the techniques they have already learned to their new and improved abilities (both physical and otherwise).

• In the second phase of puberty (adolescence), players reach full physical maturity. The body fills out more and more, offsetting increases in height. The proportions become more symmetrical, and the primary result is an improvement in coordination, both specific and general.

• The ability to retain motor skills (learning without forgetting) undergoes extensive development.

• The skeletal system's load-carrying capacity increases, reducing the risk of strain-related injury.

• Condition and coordination training should reach peak intensity at this age level (the phase of accelerated improvement in motor performance).

• The daily workout should systematically become more intense, longer, more demanding and more comprehensive (depending on your training objectives), first at a flat rate and later by stages.

• However, exertion must still always be followed by a rest period.

• Takeoff power (shooting, jumping and throwing power) and anaerobic endurance are easier to train now (but avoid incorporating your goalkeepers into your field players' special anaerobic endurance training sessions).

• To increase strength (both general and specific), you have a variety of exercises available to you.

• Exercises that protect the spine can compensate for muscular weaknesses.

• It is essential for goalkeepers to refine their techniques and learn them by heart, and to use the right technique for the situation.

• With technique, always work toward high-quality execution through precision, speed and a balance of action and relaxation.

• It is easy to practice multiple goalkeeper and field player techniques at the same time, and also to combine technique and coordination training.

• Use complex exercises and games to focus intensively on specific technical-tactical elements.

• Use practice games involving the whole team (picking up the pace and adding time and opposition pressure) to develop good technical-tactical play; this trains a goalkeeper's ability to make quick decisions.

Goalkeeper and Coach

- When making corrections, focus on specific mistakes.
- Youth goalkeeper training cannot succeed without intensive communication and cooperation between player and coach.
- Try to make every practice session intensive, focused and interesting.
- Include your goalkeepers in your practice planning; they are usually very interested in taking responsibility and helping to shape their own training.
- Individual conversations between goalkeeper and coach are more important than ever.

Oliver Kahn: winner of multiple "Player of the Year" awards and the number-one goalkeeper on Germany's national team for years is an inspiration to youth goalkeepers all over the world.

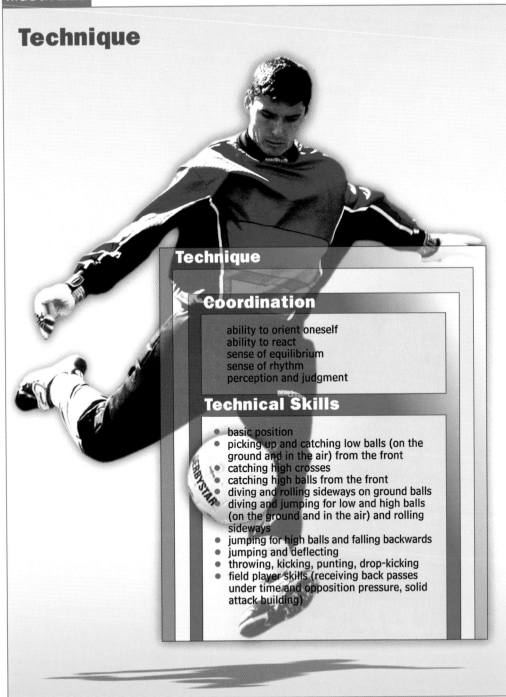

Illustr. 12a

Technique

Technique

Coordination

- ability to orient oneself
- ability to react
- sense of equilibrium
- sense of rhythm
- perception and judgment

Technical Skills

- basic position
- picking up and catching low balls (on the ground and in the air) from the front
- catching high crosses
- catching high balls from the front
- diving and rolling sideways on ground balls
- diving and jumping for low and high balls (on the ground and in the air) and rolling sideways
- jumping for high balls and falling backwards
- jumping and deflecting
- throwing, kicking, punting, drop-kicking
- field player skills (receiving back passes under time and opposition pressure, solid attack building)

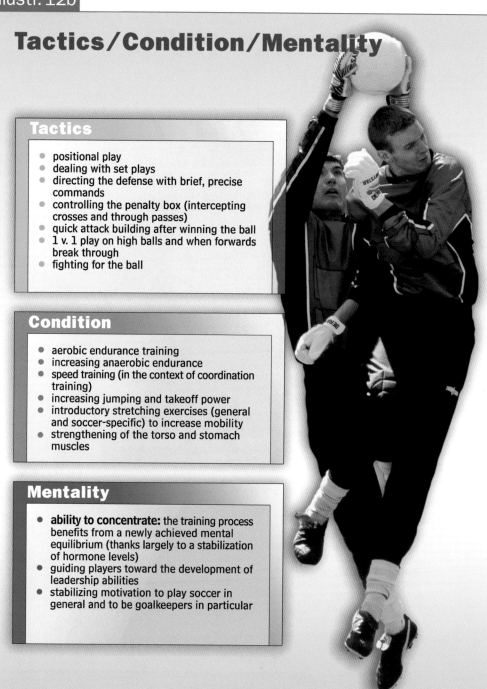

Illustr. 12b

Tactics/Condition/Mentality

Tactics

- positional play
- dealing with set plays
- directing the defense with brief, precise commands
- controlling the penalty box (intercepting crosses and through passes)
- quick attack building after winning the ball
- 1 v. 1 play on high balls and when forwards break through
- fighting for the ball

Condition

- aerobic endurance training
- increasing anaerobic endurance
- speed training (in the context of coordination training)
- increasing jumping and takeoff power
- introductory stretching exercises (general and soccer-specific) to increase mobility
- strengthening of the torso and stomach muscles

Mentality

- **ability to concentrate:** the training process benefits from a newly achieved mental equilibrium (thanks largely to a stabilization of hormone levels)
- guiding players toward the development of leadership abilities
- stabilizing motivation to play soccer in general and to be goalkeepers in particular

Illustr. 13

Age-Appropriate Warm-Up

Compared to the previous age level, warm-up for 14- to 18-year-olds is:

- more comprehensive and more intense
- more difficult
- an intensive, focused preparation for the workout to come in the main session

1. Coordination Exercises without the Ball

See warm-up program for 12- to 14-year-old goalkeepers.

2. Coordination Exercises with the Ball

See warm-up program for 12- to 14-year-old goalkeepers.

Note

- In contrast to the previous age level, you can dispense with warm-up games now. Instead, concentrate exclusively on preparing your goalkeepers for the training concepts coming up in the main session
- Every warm-up begins with running exercises without the ball for coordination. These are followed by focused stretching and strengthening exercises and coordination exercises with the ball (and possibly the coach) or an exercise from the 12- to 14-year-olds' warm-up program.

Partner Exercises

EXERCISE 1

Two goalkeepers (each one has a ball) run side by side. They simultaneously throw both balls up in the air in front of themselves, then switch sides; each catches the other's ball.

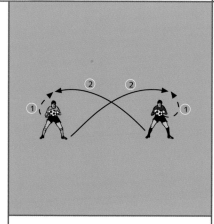

OBJECTIVES
• motivational warm-up
• developing mobility and a feel for the ball
• coordination training
• general and goalkeeper-specific technique training

VARIATIONS
1. Goalkeepers quickly tag each other before catching each other's balls.
2. Goalkeepers run side by side as above. At the coach's signal, GK1 throws one ball up in the air; GK2 hands the other to GK1 and then catches GK1's ball as GK1 switches to GK2's position (they are running very close together). At the next signal GK1 throws the ball up in the air again, GK2 hands off and catches GK1's ball on the other side.

EXERCISE 2

Two goalkeepers (each one has a ball) run side by side. At the coach's signal, they simultaneously roll their balls straight ahead, then switch sides; each dives for the other's ball.

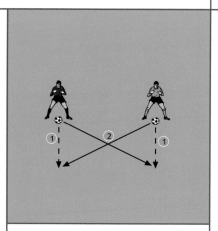

OBJECTIVE
• See Exercise 1

VARIATIONS
1. At the signal, GK1 rolls one ball straight ahead, and GK2 throws the other up in the air. Each goes for the other's ball.
2. GK2 runs behind GK1, holding a ball straight out in front with both arms extended. At the coach's signal, GK1 throws one ball up in the air, quickly turns around and touches the other ball, and turns around again and tries to catch the first ball.

EXERCISE 3

Two goalkeepers (each one has a ball) run facing each other. GK1 runs backwards, holding a ball, while GK2 runs forward dribbling. At the coach's signal, GK1 stops with legs apart and throws to GK2. GK2 passes between GK1's legs and catches GK1's ball. GK1 dives backwards for GK2's ball.

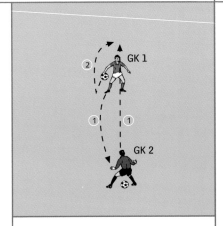

OBJECTIVE
• See Exercise 1

VARIATIONS

1. GK1 does a forward roll (or turns around once completely) before diving for the ball. GK2's pass must be carefully timed so that GK1 does not have to run too far after the ball.
2. At the signal, GK1 throws to GK2, who simultaneously passes to GK1's left or right (alternate sides); GK1 dives for the ball. Players switch roles after running a certain distance.

Running Exercises with Ball and Coach

EXERCISE 1

Two goalkeepers practice with the coach (C), who has a ball.
All three run side by side, with C in the middle. C throws the ball up in the air, and the goalkeepers take turns catching it while C tries to block them.
The group runs the same distance twice; goalkeepers take off with the left leg the first time and the right leg the second.

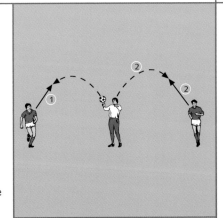

OBJECTIVES
• general warm-up
• motivational warm-up
• coordination training
• goalkeeper-specific technique training

VARIATION

Each goalkeeper must turn around once completely before catching (C tries to block as above).

EXERCISE 2

Two goalkeepers practice with the coach (C), who has a ball.

Both goalkeepers face C and run sideways. At C's signal, the right (or left) goalkeeper turns, runs forward and catches a high ball from C (who tries to block the catch).

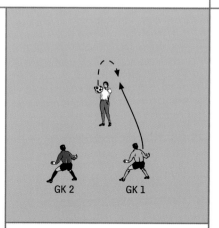

GK 2   GK 1

OBJECTIVE
● See Exercise 1

VARIATION

The goalkeeper turns and does a forward roll before catching the ball.

EXERCISE 3

Two goalkeepers practice with the coach (C), who has a ball.

Both goalkeepers run backwards. At C's signal, they stop. The front goalkeeper stands with legs apart, and the rear one crawls between them and dives for a ground ball from C.

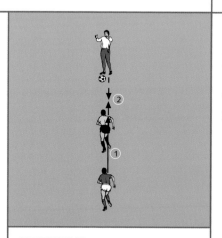

OBJECTIVE
● See Exercise 1

VARIATIONS

1. The rear goalkeeper does a forward roll before diving for the ball.
2. The front goalkeeper squats, and the rear one jumps over and catches a throw from the side.

EXERCISE 4

One goalkeeper practices with the coach (C). The goalkeeper holds a ball in both hands and runs forward, followed by C (who also has a ball). At C's signal, the goalkeeper throws the first ball up in the air and C throws the other over the goalkeeper's left (or right) shoulder. The goalkeeper instantly dives forward for C's ball, and C receives the goalkeeper's ball.

OBJECTIVE
• See Exercise 1

VARIATION

The goalkeeper runs backwards and throws to C at the signal, then dives backwards to catch C's ball.

EXERCISE 5

Two goalkeepers run, one after the other, with the coach (C) beside them.
At C's signal, the front goalkeeper does a quick backwards roll while the rear goalkeeper runs around the front one and dives for C's ground ball (or catches C's high ball) from the side.

OBJECTIVE
• See Exercise 1

VARIATION

The rear goalkeeper jumps over the front one (who is doing a backwards roll) and dives for a ground ball (or catches a high ball from the side).

Goalkeeper Techniques

Games and Exercises

In this chapter you will find practical exercises for virtually every goalkeeper technique. For each technique there are three basic exercise types, which can be changed and combined with one another. As a prerequisite, players should already have mastered the basic position and the techniques of picking up and catching low balls (on the ground and in the air) from the front and from the side.

Of course, you can also use exercises from the 12- to 14-year-old level to train 14- to 18-year-old goalkeepers, adjusting the intensity and level of difficulty to fit your players' ability level. At this age level, most goalkeeper techniques can be combined with one another as your training objectives require.

Exercise Type 1: combined technique and coordination training
Exercise Type 2: multiple player technique training
Exercise Type 3: exercises on the goal

Notes

• Coordination training should take place during warm-up and in conjunction with technique exercises.
• Certain tactics — positional play, set plays, controlling the penalty box (intercepting through passes and crosses), 1 v. 1s on high balls and against solo forwards, and winning the ball — are addressed in the third basic exercise (exercises on the goal). However, the bulk of tactics training should take place during regular sessions with the full team. Some tactics, such as organizing the defense with brief commands, can only be practiced in practice games and exercises focusing on group or team tactics. During these exercises, your job is to watch your goalkeepers and guide them in coaching their teammates. Of course, the teammates have to be involved as well ("On the field, we speak only one language.").
• 14- to 18-year-old goalkeepers should concentrate on improving the following aspects of condition:
1. aerobic and anaerobic endurance
2. speed training (in the context of coordination training)
3. jumping and takeoff power (by jumping over objects or players and executing a follow-up play with the ball)
4. mobility (with general and soccer-specific stretching exercises)
5. torso and stomach muscles (working against one's own body weight, also with partner exercises and light weights).
• Also work on improving players' attitude toward the game and their willingness to get involved.

Catching High Balls from the Front and from the Side

Technique and Coordination

BASIC EXERCISE 1A

The goalkeeper juggles a ball at a cone; the coach (C) stands five yards away. At C's signal, the goalkeeper passes the ball to C, does a forward roll and then catches a high ball thrown by C.

VARIATIONS

1. C acts as an active opponent.
2. The goalkeeper juggles the ball two yards away from the cone. At C's signal, the goalkeeper passes to C, does a backwards roll, runs backwards to the cone and forward around it, and does another forward roll before catching the high ball from C.

FOCUS ON:

- swinging the arms for more momentum on the jump
- extending the arms forward or upward toward the ball, keeping the wrists firm and spreading the fingers wide

BASIC EXERCISE 1B

The goalkeeper juggles at cone A, with two more cones five yards ahead to the left and right. The coach (C) stands 10 yards away. At C's signal ("left" or "right"), the goalkeeper passes to C, does a forward roll toward the designated cone and touches it. Then the goalkeeper runs backwards back to Cone A, facing C. Suddenly C throws a high ball to the goalkeeper, who stops running and catches it.

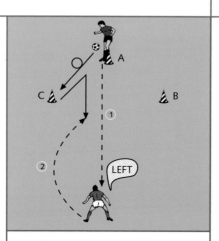

FOCUS ON
● See Exercise 1A

VARIATION

The goalkeeper stands at Cone B. At C's signal, the goalkeeper quickly turns around once completely and then catches a high ball thrown by C. The goalkeeper throws it back and runs around Cone C, then does a forward roll toward Cone A, runs around it, and imme-diately runs for a ground ball from C (aimed at Cone B). The goalkeeper dives to the left for the ball.
Then the exercise starts over with the goalkeeper at Cone C.

Multiple Player Technique Training

BASIC EXERCISE 2A

Cones A, B and C form a triangle (15 yards on each side). A goalkeeper stands at each cone. GK1 holds one ball; another is at GK3's feet. At a signal from the coach (C), GK1 throws a high ball to GK2, who catches it. At the same time GK3 passes on the ground to GK1, who quickly turns to face GK3 and stops the ball. Then GK2 throws a high ball to GK3 and stops a ground ball from GK1, etc. When C calls out "switch," players start passing in the opposite direction.

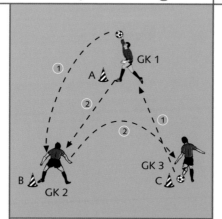

FOCUS ON:
● General field player skills
● keeping the arms bent and pulling the ball in to the body when receiving
● always taking off with only one leg

VARIATIONS

1. Now GK2 has a ball on the ground as well. At C's signal, all three goalkeepers pass simultaneously: GK1 throws a high ball to GK2, GK2 passes on the ground to GK3, and GK3 passes on the ground to GK1. When C calls out "switch," they start passing in the opposite direction.
2. Only GK3 passes on the ground; the others pass in the air.

BASIC EXERCISE 2B

Cones A, B and C form a triangle (five yards on each side). A goalkeeper stands at each cone. At C's signal, each goalkeeper throws a ball up in the air and immediately rotates clockwise to the next cone, then tries to catch the previous player's ball. When C calls out "switch," players start passing in the opposite direction.

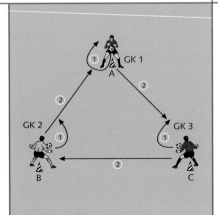

FOCUS ON
• See Exercise 2A

VARIATIONS

1. Goalkeepers bounce their balls hard on the ground and rotate clockwise.
2. Each player volleys to the next one (clockwise), who catches it high in the air. When C calls out "switch," they start volleying in the opposite direction.
3. Each player drop-kicks to the next one (clockwise) and proceeds as above.

Exercises on the Goal

BASIC EXERCISE 3A

Two goalkeepers (GK1 and GK2) practice with the coach (C). GK1 stands at a cone in a standard goal with a ball held between the knees. GK2 stands at a cone 16 yards in front of the goal. The coach (C) has a ball and stands at or near the penalty box corner. At C's signal, GK1 does a forward roll, releases the ball and passes it to GK2, then runs backwards to the cone in the goal and around it. Then C throws a high ball. GK1 catches it and rolls it back, and GK2 tries to score against GK1 with an instep shot.

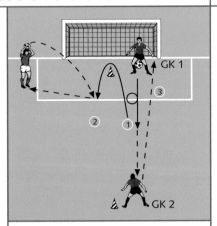

NOTES
• C throws high balls in front of the goal from both sides.
• Players switch roles and positions if one of them scores, or after several rounds.

VARIATION

GK2 has a ball instead of C. GK1 does a backwards roll, releases the ball and passes it to C, then turns to face GK2, who throws a high ball toward the goal. GK1 catches it and rolls it back to GK2, then turns back toward C, who shoots on the ground at the near corner of the goal. GK1 dives to the side for the ball. Note: C shoots from both sides, alternating every time, more or less.

BASIC EXERCISE 3B

Starting positions are the same as in Exercise 3A, except C has two balls and GK1 has none.

At C's signal, GK1 does a forward roll and catches a high ball, throws it to GK2 and does another forward roll toward GK2, who tries to score with a drop-kick. GK1 blocks the shot and turns back toward C, who shoots the second ball at the near corner. Once again, GK1 tries to block the shot.

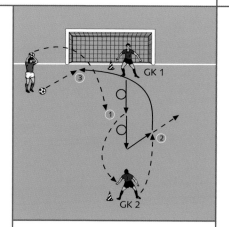

NOTES
• See Exercise 3A

BASIC EXERCISE 3C

The coach (C) practices with three goalkeepers. Two standard goals face one another across a 20 x 15-yard field (marked by cones). GK1 and GK2 stand in the goals, while C and GK3 stand behind opposite sidelines with one ball each. GK3 kicks a high ball in front of GK1's goal, and GK1 catches it and throws it to C on the other side. C kicks a high ball in front of the other goal, where GK2 catches it and throws it to GK3. The exercise starts over again from the beginning.

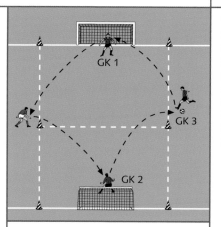

VARIATIONS
1. After GK1 catches the ball and throws it to C, C kicks a high ball back to GK1. In other words, each goalkeeper catches two high balls in a row, one from the left and one from the right.
2. C and GK3 punt, volley or drop-kick at the goals.

NOTE
• Players switch roles and positions after several rounds.

Diving and Rolling Sideways on Ground Balls

Technique and Coordination

BASIC EXERCISE 1A

Four cones (A–D) form a square (three yards on each side). The goalkeeper stands in the square, next to cone B. The coach (C) has a ball and stands five yards outside the square. At C's signal, the goalkeeper runs forward to Cone C and around it, then backwards (outside the square) back to Cone B. Then the goalkeeper dives toward Cone A for a ground ball from C.
Then the exercise starts over again with the goalkeeper standing next to Cone A.

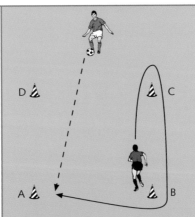

FOCUS ON
- rolling over the hips, side and shoulder
- reaching for the ball with both hands
- getting one hand behind the ball and the other on (or behind) it

VARIATIONS
1. The goalkeeper starts the exercise with a forward roll.
2. The goalkeeper does a backwards roll before running backwards.
3. The goalkeeper starts out lying face down, head toward C, in the center of the square. C points toward a cone (A or B), and the goalkeeper runs backwards around it, then dives to the side for a ground ball from C. If the goalkeeper runs around Cone A, then C passes toward Cone B, and vice versa.

BASIC EXERCISE 1B

Set up the same square as in Exercise 1A. The goalkeeper stands outside the square next to Cone C. The coach (C) has a ball and stands four yards outside the square. First the goalkeeper dives to the right for a ground ball thrown by C and throws it back while still lying on the ground. Then the goalkeeper stands up, runs around Cone B, does a forward roll toward Cone C and stands up. C throws a ball into the square, and the goalkeeper tries to catch it before it hits the ground. Finally, the goalkeeper dives for another ground ball on the left.

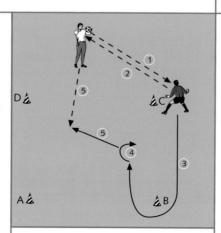

FOCUS ON
• See Exercise 1A

VARIATIONS
1. C throws a high ball to one side of the goalkeeper, who catches it.
2. After running around Cone B, the goalkeeper does a backwards (not forward) roll. Then C throws a low ball to the goalkeeper's left.

Multiple Player Technique Training

BASIC EXERCISE 2A

GK1 stands in Goal A (six yards wide), four yards behind Goal B (two yards wide). GK2 has a ball and stands five yards in front of Goal B. The coach (C) has another ball and stands four yards to the side of Goal B. At C's signal, GK1 runs toward Goal B. GK2 kicks a ball on the ground through Goal B to GK1, who passes it directly back through Goal B with the inside of the left (or right) foot. The GK1 turns toward C and dives toward Goal A for another ground ball.

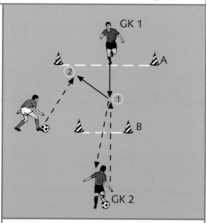

FOCUS ON
• practicing on both sides (players switch roles and positions after several rounds)
• always keeping your eyes on the ball

VARIATIONS
1. GK1 does a forward roll before running to Goal B.
2. GK1 passes GK2's ground ball back, then does a backwards roll before diving for C's ground ball.
3. C starts the exercise with a ground ball to GK1, who passes it directly back with the inside of the left (or right) foot. Then the exercise proceeds as above.

BASIC EXERCISE 2B

Three cones (A–C) form a triangle (three yards on each side). A goalkeeper stands at each cone (GK1 at A, GK2 at B, and GK3 at C). GK1 holds one ball, and another rests at GK3's feet. At the coach's signal, GK1 throws the first ball up in the air, and GK3 kicks a ground ball toward Cone B at the same time. GK2 runs to Cone A and catches GK1's ball. GK1 runs to Cone B and dives to the side for GK3's ball. Then GK2 throws the first ball up in the air and runs to Cone C while GK1 kicks a ground ball toward Cone C. GK2 dives for that ball, and GK3 catches the other at Cone A, etc.

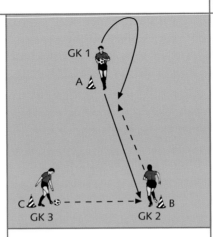

VARIATIONS

1. Players bounce their balls hard on the ground instead of throwing them up in the air.
2. Players do forward rolls before diving for balls on the ground. The player kicking the ground ball has to delay it slightly.

NOTES

- Running paths should be determined in advance to keep players from running into each other.
- When the coach calls out, "switch," players start passing in the opposite direction.

BASIC EXERCISE 2C

Two five-yard-wide goals (A and B) stand facing each other, eight yards apart. There are four goalkeepers (GK1–4); GK2 and GK4 each have a ball. GK1 and GK3 start out in push-up position facing the left posts of their goals. GK2 stands directly behind GK1, GK4 behind GK3. At the coach's (C's) signal, GK2 and GK4 pass under their partners toward the opposite goals. GK1 and GK3 immediately start toward the balls and dive for them (to the left). GK2 and GK4 each move to the other post, and the exercise starts over again.

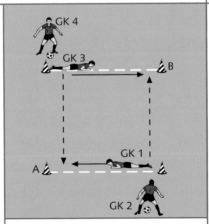

VARIATION

GK1 and GK3 lie face down, heads toward the right posts. GK2 and GK4 each have a ball and stand directly to the right of GK1 and GK3, respectively. At C's signal, GK2 and GK4 pass on the ground toward the opposite goals. GK1 and GK3 start toward the balls and dive for them (to the left).

NOTE

- Players switch roles and positions after several rounds.

Exercises on the Goal

BASIC EXERCISE 3A

GK1 and GK2 practice with the coach (C). To the left and right of a standard goal are two five-yard-wide goals (A and B). Two more goals (C and D) stand opposite A and B on the penalty box line, with a ball in the center of each. GK2 lies between Goals C and D with a cone three yards away on the left. GK1 stands in the big goal, and C has a ball and stands five yards in front of it. C kicks a ground ball to one side of GK1. As soon as GK1 dives for it, GK2 gets up, runs around the cone, runs to one of the balls in Goals C and D and finishes with an instep shot.

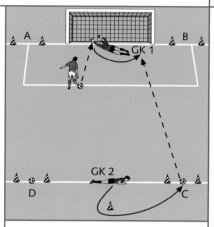

NOTE

- Goalkeepers switch roles and positions if GK2 scores, or after several rounds.

VARIATION

GK1 starts out in push-up position in Goal A, head toward the big goal. GK2 is in push-up position in Goal D. At C's signal, GK1 gets up, runs toward the big goal for a ground ball from C, dives to the left, rolls the ball back while still lying on the ground and then gets up. At the same time, GK2 heads for the ball in Goal C and tries to score against GK1 with a left instep shot.

Then the exercise starts over again, but GK1 starts in Goal B and dives to the right for C's ground ball. GK2 starts in Goal C and runs for the ball in Goal D.

BASIC EXERCISE 3B

Setup is as above.
GK1 lies face down in Goal A, head toward the big goal. GK2 lies in Goal B. The coach (C) has a ball and stands four yards beyond Goal B. At C's signal, GK1 and GK2 get up. GK2 dives to the left for a ground ball from C, while GK1 runs once around the left post of Goal A and then moves to the big goal to await GK2's shot. GK2 gets up, rolls the ball a short distance forward and finishes with a right instep shot.

NOTES

- See Exercise 3A.
- Practice on both sides (alternating between Goals A and B and Goals C and D).

VARIATIONS

1. Goalkeepers start out kneeling with their hands clasped behind their backs.
2. Both goalkeepers start out by running around the right posts of their goals; otherwise everything is as above.

Diving and Jumping for High and Low Balls and Rolling Sideways

Technique and Coordination

BASIC EXERCISE 1A

Set up a row of cones in the center of a seven-yard-wide goal. The goalkeeper starts out in push-up position to the left of the cones, facing the coach (C). C has a ball and stands three yards in front of the cones. The goalkeeper does a push-up and jumps over the cones for a low (or high) throw from C. Then the goalkeeper goes back into push-up position on the right side of the cones, does two push-ups and jumps back over the cones for another low (or high) throw from C.

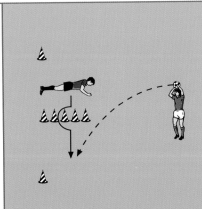

NOTE
• Each series consists of 2 x 3 jumps over the cones. The goalkeeper does one push-up before the first jump, two before the second and finally three before the third.

VARIATIONS
1. The goalkeeper starts out facing the cones and does a push-up, gets up, runs backwards around the near goalpost and then jumps over the cones for the ball as above.
2. The goalkeeper stands to the left of the cones. At C's signal, the goalkeeper jumps over them and passes a ground ball from C directly back with the inside of the right foot, then touches the right goalpost and jumps back over the cone for a throw from C.

BASIC EXERCISE 1B

Set up a row of cones in the center of a six-yard-wide goal. The goalkeeper starts out in push-up position at one end of the row; the coach (C) has a ball and stands three yards beyond the other. The goalkeeper crawls sideways along the row toward C. If C calls out "forward," the goalkeeper does a forward roll, gets up, touches the right post and jumps back over the cones for a ball from C. If C calls out "back," the goalkeeper pushes off hard from the ground and stands up, runs backwards around the left post, runs forward and jumps over the cones for the ball.

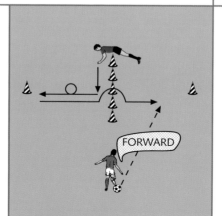

FORWARD

VARIATION

If the coach calls out "back," the goalkeeper does a backwards roll first.

FOCUS ON

- swinging the arms
- shifting the center of gravity over the takeoff leg
- explosive lift with the takeoff leg (brief contact with the ground)
- accelerating directly toward the ball

Multiple Player Technique Training

BASIC EXERCISE 2A

Two goalkeepers (GK1 and GK2) practice with the coach (C). GK1 sits next to a row of cones in the center of a six-yard-wide goal. GK2 stands four yards in front of the left post, C in front of the right post; each one has a ball. At C's signal, GK1 does a backwards roll and stands up. Then GK2 kicks a ground ball at GK1, who receives and controls it with the right foot, then passes it back to GK2 with the inside of the left foot. Then GK1 touches the left post and jumps over the cones for a throw from C.

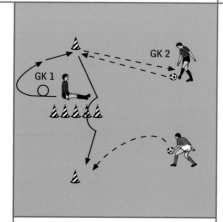

GK 2

GK 1

NOTE

- Players switch roles and positions after several rounds.

VARIATIONS

1. GK2 has two balls and throws the first to GK1. GK1 catches it and rolls backwards while holding it in both hands; drops it behind his head, rolls forward and stands up. Then GK2 passes the second ball on the ground to GK1's left. GK1 deflects it to the side, gets up and jumps over the cones for a ball from C.

2. GK2 has one ball and throws it to GK1, who catches it, rolls backwards and then rolls forward again, still holding it. GK1 throws it to GK2 while rolling and stands up. GK2 throws the ball to GK1, who volleys it back with the left foot, then jumps over the cones for C's ball.

BASIC EXERCISE 2B

Setup is as above. GK1 lays face down to the left of the cones, feet toward GK2, who has a ball and stands four yards in front of GK1. The coach (C) also has a ball and stands two yards in front of the goal, to the right of the cones. At C's signal, GK1 gets up and runs around the cones toward C. As soon as GK1 reaches the goal line, C kicks a ground ball, which GK1 passes back with the inside of the right foot. Then GK1 jumps over the cones for a throw from GK2.

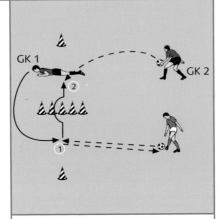

FOCUS ON/NOTES

- switching roles and positions after several rounds
- fast, explosive takeoff toward the ball
- jumping straight toward the ball

VARIATION

At C's signal, GK1 rolls to the left and gets up. GK2 kicks a ground ball, which GK1 passes back precisely with the inside of the left foot. Then GK1 runs backwards to the end of the row and forward around it. When GK1 reaches the end of the row, C kicks a ground ball; GK1 passes it back with the inside of the right foot and jumps over the cones for another ball from GK2.

Exercises on the Goal

BASIC EXERCISE 3A

Set up a row of cones in front of a standard goal. GK1 stands to the left of the cones. GK2 stands four yards in front of GK1, the coach behind the row and to the right; each of them has a ball. GK1 passes GK2's ground ball back with the inside of the left foot and jumps over the cones for a throw from C. Then GK1 passes a ground ball from C back with the inside of the right foot and jumps over the cones for a throw from GK2.

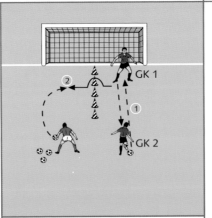

FOCUS ON/NOTES

- See Exercise 2B
- Players should pause between jumps

VARIATIONS

1. GK2 throws a low ball to GK1, who volleys it back before jumping over the cones for the next ball.
2. GK2 throws a high ball to GK1, who receives it on the chest or knee and volleys it back, then jumps over the cones.

BASIC EXERCISE 3B

The coach (C) has a ball and stands in front of the cones on the right. GK1 stands just left of the cones; GK2 has a ball and stands four yards in front of GK1. GK2 passes the ball so that by diving, GK1 can either pass it back or deflect it to the side with the right foot. Then GK1 quickly gets up, turns toward C and jumps over the cones for a low (or high) throw from C.

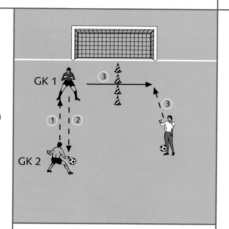

FOCUS ON/NOTES
- See Exercise 2B

BASIC EXERCISE 3C

The goalkeeper stands on the left, near the right post of a standard goal and just to the right of a row of three cones (spaced one yard apart). The coach (C) has a ball and stands five yards in front of the goal. The goalkeeper does two-legged sideways jumps in a zigzag pattern over the cones, then dives to the left for a throw from C.

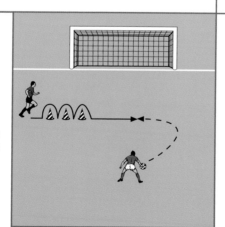

FOCUS ON
- taking off explosively with both legs
- taking a short sideways step and jumping for the ball

VARIATION

The goalkeeper stands facing the coach and slaloms through the cones, running forward and backwards, taking quick, short steps.

Jumping to Deflect High Balls and Falling Backwards

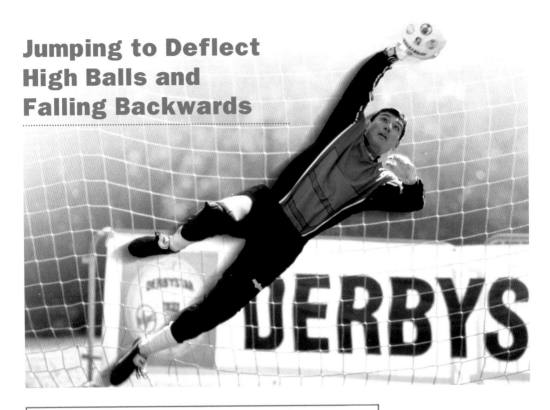

Technique and Coordination

BASIC EXERCISE 1

The goalkeeper stands seven yards in front of a standard goal and faces the coach (C), who has several balls. C throws the balls up in the air so that the goalkeeper can deflect them over the goal, using the right hand.

FOCUS ON
- keeping your eyes on the ball
- turning quickly to face the goal or ball
- taking a long stride toward the ball on the last step

VARIATIONS

1. C throws the ball up so that the goalkeeper has to run a short distance in order to deflect it over the goal. The goalkeeper then goes directly into a forward roll.
2. C throws the ball so that the goalkeeper has to jump for it.

Multiple Player Technique Training

BASIC EXERCISE 2A

Two goalkeepers practice with the coach (C). GK1 sits on the ground, three yards in front of GK2 and three yards behind C, who has a ball. C throws the ball to GK1, who falls back sideways and deflects the ball to GK2 with the right hand (reaching overhead to do so – see the section on deflecting in Chapter 2). GK2 catches the ball and throws it back to C, and the exercise starts over again. This time, GK1 deflects the ball to GK2 with the left hand.

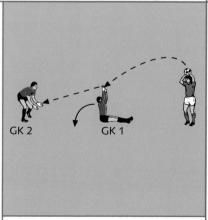

GK 2   GK 1

NOTE
● Goalkeepers switch roles and positions after several rounds.

VARIATIONS

1. GK1 starts out standing, and C and GK2 stand farther away. C throws a high ball to GK1, who deflects it to GK2 with the right (or left) hand from the standing position.
2. Players stand even farther apart. C throws a high ball to GK1, who falls back sideways and deflects it to GK2 with the right (or left) hand.
3. GK1 does a forward roll to a cone and touches it before falling back sideways and deflecting the ball to GK2.

BASIC EXERCISE 2B

Two goalkeepers practice with the coach (C). GK1 sits in the center of a seven-yard-wide goal. C has two balls and stands five yards in front of it, and GK2 stands five yards behind it. C throws a high ball to GK1, who deflects it to GK2 with the right (or left) hand, then quickly gets up and dives to the right (or left) side for a ground ball from C.

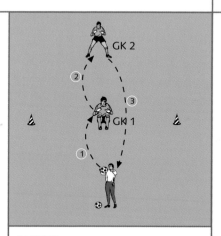

GK 2

GK 1

NOTES
● See Exercise 2A

BASIC EXERCISE 2C

Setup is as above, except GK1 starts out standing in the goal.

The coach (C) throws a high ball in front of GK1, who jumps up to punch it back to C with both fists, then immediately does a backwards roll toward the goal, gets up quickly, falls back and deflects a second ball from C to GK2 with the right (or left) hand.

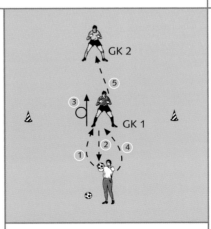

VARIATION

GK1 stands facing away from C. At C's signal, GK1 does a backwards roll, gets up and turns to face C. C throws a high ball over GK1, who falls back and deflects it to GK2 with the right (or left) hand.

NOTE
- Players switch roles and positions after several rounds.

Exercises on the Goal

BASIC EXERCISE 3A

Two goalkeepers (GK1 and GK2) practice with the coach (C). GK1 stands in the center of a standard goal, with a cone six yards in front and to the left. GK2 stands directly to the right of the goal; C has several balls and stands 10 yards in front of it. At C's signal, GK1 does a forward roll, touches the cone and then turns to the right. As soon as GK1 touches the cone, C throws a high ball over GK1 toward the right corner of the goal. GK1 runs toward the goal, jumps up and deflects the ball to GK2 beside the goal, using the left hand.

NOTE
- GK1 switches with GK2 after several rounds. Once both of them have practiced, they practice deflecting with the right hand (move the cone to the goalkeeper's right).

VARIATION

GK1 stands five yards in front of the goal, GK2 behind it. C has several balls and stands five yards in front of GK1. C kicks a ground ball to the left of GK2, who dives for it, throws it back to C while still lying on the ground, and gets up. Then C throws a high ball over GK1 toward the goal. GK1 runs for the ball and deflects it over the goal to GK2, using the left hand. GK1 returns to the starting position, and C kicks a ground ball to the right. They proceed as above, except this time GK1 uses the right hand to deflect the ball over the goal. GK2 catches the balls and throws them back to C.

BASIC EXERCISE 3B

Two goalkeepers (GK1 and GK2) practice with the coach (C). GK1 stands at the right post of a standard goal, GK2 left of the left post. C has a ball and stands six yards in front of the goal. At C's signal, GK1 turns left 270 degrees and runs for a high ball from C aimed at the left corner of the goal. GK1 jumps up and deflects the ball to GK2 beside the goal, using the right hand (reaching overhead to do so).

VARIATION

GK1 stands to the right of the right post, facing away from C. At C's signal, GK1 turns to the right and runs for a throw from C aimed at the left corner of the goal.

NOTE
- Goalkeepers switch after several rounds. Once both of them have practiced, C aims at the right corner of the goal, and goalkeepers deflect with the left hand.

BASIC EXERCISE 3C

GK1 stands in the center of a standard goal, GK2 left of the left post. The coach (C) has several balls and stands six yards in front of it. C kicks the first ball on the ground at the left post. GK1 runs for the ball, slides and kicks it to GK2 with the right foot, quickly gets up again and runs for another ground ball from C aimed at the right post. GK1 dives to the right for the ball, deflects it to the side, rolls over and then starts running for a third ball from C thrown at the left corner of the goal. GK1 deflects it to GK2 with the right hand.

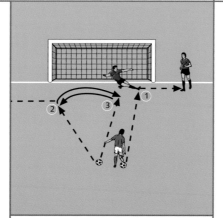

VARIATIONS

1. First C throws a low ball at the left post, and GK1 volleys it to GK2.
2. First C throws a high ball at the left post, and GK1 heads it to GK2.

NOTE
- Goalkeepers switch roles and positions after several rounds.

Jumping and Deflecting (Punching Out)

Technique and Coordination

BASIC EXERCISE 1A

Two goalkeepers (GK1 and GK2) practice with the coach (C). GK1 stands in a small goal (five yards wide). GK2 stands behind it, and C has a ball and stands 10 yards in front of it. C throws a high ball to GK1, who punches it back to C with both fists (standing still).

Afterwards GK1 and GK2 switch positions, and the exercise starts over again.

FOCUS ON

- taking off with one leg (the leg closer to the ball): right leg on balls from the right, and vice-versa
- powerful takeoff from the ground, swinging the arms and the other leg up (also for protection)

VARIATIONS

1. C throws a high ball to GK2, who jumps up to punch it back with both fists. Afterwards the goalkeepers switch positions, and the exercise starts over again.

2. At C's signal, GK2 does a backwards roll, stands up and jumps up to punch a high ball back to C with both fists. GK1 acts as a semi-active opponent. Then the goalkeepers switch positions, and the exercise starts over again.

BASIC EXERCISE 1B

Two goalkeepers practice with the coach (C). GK1 stands in a small goal (five yards wide) four yards in front of GK2. C has a ball and stands 10 yards in front of them.

At C's signal, GK2 does a forward roll, stands up and jumps up to punch a high ball back to C with both fists. GK1 acts as a semi-active opponent. Then the goalkeepers switch positions, and the exercise starts over again.

FOCUS ON
• See Exercise 1A

VARIATION
GK1 is on hands and knees; GK2 jumps over and punches a high ball back to C with both fists. Then GK2 runs backwards behind GK1, and the exercise starts over again.

Multiple Player Technique Training

BASIC EXERCISE 2A

Three cones form a triangle (10 yards on each side). A goalkeeper stands at each cone; GK1 has a ball. GK1 throws a high ball to GK2, who turns toward GK3 and punches it in that direction with both fists. GK3 catches the ball and throws it to GK1, who turns toward GK2 and punches the ball in that direction with both fists, etc.

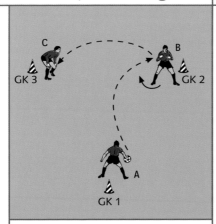

NOTE
• After several rounds, players stop catching and simply punch the ball.

VARIATIONS
1. Players switch directions at C's signal.
2. One goalkeeper (GK2) practices punching, and the other two act as throwers (each has a supply of balls). GK1 throws a high ball to GK2, who jumps up to punch it back with both fists. Then GK2 turns toward GK3 and jumps up to punch another high ball back. GK2 switches positions with another goalkeeper after several rounds.

BASIC EXERCISE 2B

Three cones form a triangle (10 yards on each side). A goalkeeper stands at each cone; GK1 has a ball. GK1 throws a high ball to GK2, who jumps up and punches it to GK3 with both fists. GK3 catches it, and the exercise starts over again. Players switch roles after several rounds.

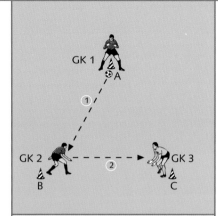

VARIATIONS

1. GK3 holds a ball; GK1 has one on the ground. GK1 passes on the ground to GK2, who passes back with the inside of the right foot, then turns and jumps up to punch a high ball back to GK3 with both fists. Players switch roles after several rounds.
2. GK1 throws a low ball to GK2, who volleys it back with the right foot.

FOCUS ON

- straightening the arm quickly (but not completely); hitting the ball at the highest point possible as the fist moves diagonally from low inside to high center

Exercises on the Goal

BASIC EXERCISE 3A

Three goalkeepers (GK1–3) practice with the coach (C). GK1 stands in a standard goal. C stands 15 yards away at the inside right, GK2 stands in the middle and GK3 stands at the inside left; C and GK3 each have a ball. C throws a high ball to GK1, who jumps up and punches it to GK2 with both fists. GK2 catches the ball and throws it to GK1, who punches it back to C. Then GK3 throws a high ball from the side to GK1, who punches it to GK2. GK2 catches the ball and throws it back to GK1, who punches it back to GK3. Then the exercise starts over again.

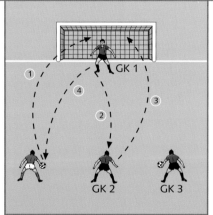

VARIATION

GK2 has a ball; the others do not. GK2 throws a high ball to GK1, who punches it to C with the left fist. C catches the ball and throws it to GK1, who punches it back to GK2 with both fists. GK2 catches the ball and throws it back to GK1, who punches it to GK3 with the right fist. GK3 catches the ball and throws it back to GK1, who punches it back to GK2 with both fists. Then GK2 starts the exercise over again.

NOTE

- Players switch roles and positions after several rounds.

BASIC EXERCISE 3B

Setup is the same as in Exercise 3A, except now GK2 and GK3 have one ball each. GK2 kicks a ground ball to the left of GK1, who dives for the ball and throws it back to GK2 while still lying on the ground. Then GK1 gets up and punches a high ball from the side back to C with both fists, and returns to the goal and assumes the basic position. GK2 kicks a ground ball to the right of GK1, and the exercise starts over again. This time GK3 throws the high ball from the side for to GK1 to punch.

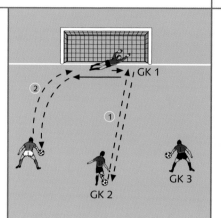

NOTE
• See Exercise 3A

VARIATION

GK2 passes on the ground to GK1, who passes the ball back on the ground with the inside of the right foot. Then GK3 throws a high ball to GK1, and GK1 punches it to C with the left fist. GK2 kicks another ground ball to GK1, who passes it back and then punches a high ball from the other side back to GK3 with the right fist.

BASIC EXERCISE 3C

Three goalkeepers (GK1–3) practice with the coach (C). GK1 stands in a standard goal. C and GK3 stand 15 yards away, C at the inside left and GK3 at the inside right; C has a ball. GK2 is directly in front of the goal, about eight yards away. C kicks a high ball from the side in front of the goal. GK1 punches it to GK3 with the left fist. Then GK3 kicks a high ball in front of the goal from the other side, and GK1 punches it to C with the right fist, etc. GK2 does not interfere, initially.

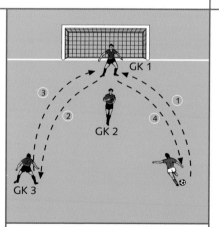

NOTE
• See Exercise 3A

VARIATION

GK2 tries to score on the high balls with headers.

Throwing, Kicking, Punting, Drop-Kicking

The most important part of kicking, throwing, punting and drop-kicking is to get the ball to a *teammate*.

Technique and Coordination

BASIC EXERCISE 1

The goalkeeper stands five yards in front of a hurdle with a small goal (five yards wide) one yard beyond it. The coach (C) stands 10 yards beyond the goal. The goalkeeper drop-kicks to C, then jumps over the hurdle and dives to the left or right for a ground ball from C. The goalkeeper tries to reach the ball before it crosses the goal line.

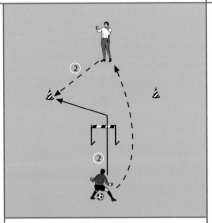

NOTE
• At this age level, exercises should always combine several techniques, unless players are having serious problems with specific ones.

VARIATION

The goalkeeper throws the ball to C.

Multiple Player Technique Training

BASIC EXERCISE 2A

Three goalkeepers (GK1–3) practice together. GK1 has a ball and stands in a small goal (five yards wide). GK2 stands about 10 yards in front of the goal, GK3 10 yards past GK2. GK1 drop-kicks to GK2, who catches the ball and drop-kicks it back. Then GK1 drop-kicks to GK3 and switches positions with GK2. GK3 catches the ball and drop-kicks it to GK1, who catches it and drop-kicks it back to GK3. GK3 drop-kicks to GK2 and switches positions with GK1; GK2 catches the ball and drop-kicks it to GK3, who catches it and drop-kicks it back. GK2 drop-kicks to GK1 and switches positions with GK3, etc.

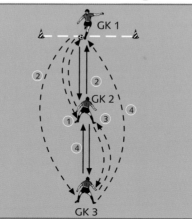

FOCUS ON

- catching the ball in front of the body
- keeping the ankle firm and the toes pointing downward
- pointing the toes of the standing foot in the direction of the kick

VARIATIONS

1. GK1 punts (or volleys) a high ball to GK2, who catches it and throws it back. Then GK1 punts (or volleys) to GK3 and switches positions with GK2. GK3 catches the ball and volleys it back to GK1, who catches it and throws it back to GK3. Then GK3 punts (or volleys) to GK2 and switches positions with GK1, etc.
2. Sequence is as above, except players stand farther apart and do not switch positions.

BASIC EXERCISE 2B

Setup is as above, except now GK2 stands 20 yards in front of the goal, and GK3 20 yards past GK2.
GK1 passes to GK3 with a precise instep kick and immediately switches positions with GK2. GK3 receives the ball like a back pass, then passes to GK2 with a precise instep kick and switches positions with GK1, etc.

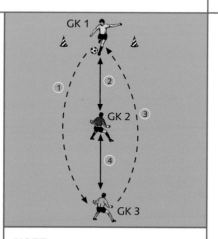

NOTE

- This exercise is best with four goalkeepers (less intense physically).

BASIC EXERCISE 2C

Four goalkeepers (GK1–4) practice together. Each one stands in a small goal (A–D, each six yards wide). Goals A and B face each other, 40 yards apart, and so do C and D. GK1 (in Goal A) and GK3 (in C) have one ball each. GK1 and GK3 simultaneously drop-kick at the opposite goals. GK2 and GK4 receive the balls and drop-kick them back.

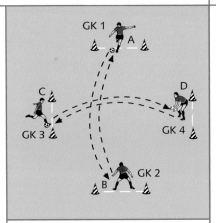

VARIATIONS

1. Players punt instead of drop-kicking.
2. Players kick, and they receive the kicks like back passes.
3. Each goalkeeper has a ball, and they all pass to their partners at the same time.

FOCUS ON

- catching the ball in front of the body
- keeping the ankle firm and the toes pointing downward
- pointing the toes of the standing foot in the direction of the kick

Exercises on the Goal

BASIC EXERCISE 3A

Two goalkeepers (GK1 and GK2) practice with the coach (C). GK1 stands in a standard goal, GK2 stands on the centerline, and C stands 25 yards in front of the goal at the inside left; GK1 and C have one ball each. GK1 kicks the ball to GK2 from the goal box line, and GK2 catches it in the air. Then C kicks a high ball in front of the goal. GK1 catches it and throws it back to C. GK2 drop-kicks another high ball in front of the goal. GK1 catches it and lays it back on the goal box line, and the exercise starts over again.

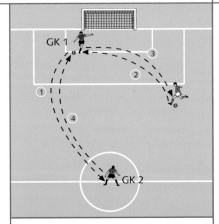

VARIATION

GK2 stands about 35 yards in front of the goal to the left, and C stands directly in front of the goal, 20 yards away. Neither one has a ball. GK1 kicks a high ball to GK2, who receives it like a back pass and sends it back in front of the goal with a high, precise instep kick. GK1 deflects the ball to C with both fists. C tries to score against GK1 with an instep kick. Then GK1 starts the next round with a precise kick to GK2.

NOTE

- Goalkeepers switch positions after several rounds. Once both of them have practiced, C switches to the other side, and the exercise starts over again with GK1 in the goal.

BASIC EXERCISE 3B

Two goalkeepers (GK1 and GK2) practice with the coach (C). GK1 stands in a standard goal, GK2 stands 35 yards away at the inside left, and C stands 25 yards away, directly in front of the goal. C has two balls and throws one up in the air in front of the goal. GK1 catches it and throws it to GK2.
Then C throws the second ball over GK1 toward the goal. GK1 goes after the ball and deflects it over or beside the goal, using the right or left hand. Finally, GK2 kicks the other ball back to C with an instep kick.

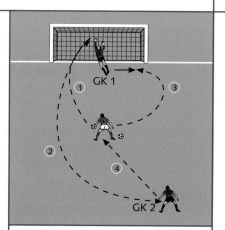

NOTE

- Goalkeepers switch positions after several rounds. Once both of them have practiced, GK2 moves to the inside right.

BASIC EXERCISE 3C

Three goalkeepers (GK1–3) practice with the coach (C). GK1 stands in a standard goal. GK2 and GK3 have one ball each and stand just out-side the left and right side-lines. C has a ball and stands 16 yards in front of the goal. First GK2 drop-kicks a high ball in front of the goal. GK1 catches it and drop-kicks it back. Then C kicks a high ball in front of the goal. GK1 catches it and throws it back to C. Then GK3 drop-kicks a high ball in front of the goal. GK1 catches it and drop-kicks it back to GK3, etc.

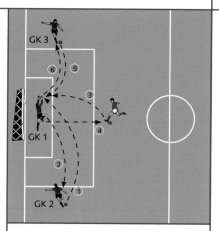

NOTE

- After several rounds, GK1 switches positions with one of the other goal-keepers.

VARIATION

GK2 and GK3 kick high balls in front of the goal. GK1 catches them and throws precisely back to the passers.

Sample Practice Session

Technique Training

Notes on Organization
Practice Time: 70–80 minutes
Group Size: 3–4 goalkeepers
Equipment: 10 balls, cones or other markers, two standard goals (or one standard goal and one five-yard-wide goal)

Focus On:
- catching low balls from the front
- catching high crosses
- catching high balls from the front
- diving and rolling sideways on ground balls
- diving/jumping for low and high balls, and rolling sideways
- jumping and deflecting

- field player skills: receiving back passes under time and opposition pressure (solid attack building)

Warm-Up:
- coordination: running exercises without the ball
- coordination: running exercises with ball and coach

Practice Time: 15–20 minutes

Catching High Balls from the Front

EXERCISE
Four goalkeepers practice together. Two of them (in small goals) drop-kick back and forth; the other two do coordination exercises with the ball. After these two have run a certain distance, players switch roles.

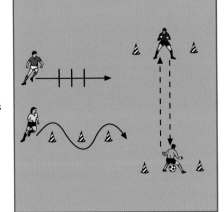

NOTES
- Catching high balls from the front is a skill that should normally be practiced during warm-up.
- You can also do this exercise with only three goalkeepers.

Falling and Rolling on Ground Balls

EXERCISE

GK1 stands in a standard goal, GK2 at the left (or right) post. At the coach's (C's) signal, GK1 does a sideways roll (over the shoulders) toward GK2, quickly tags GK2 and immediately starts running in the opposite direction for a ground ball from C.

NOTES

- Players switch roles after three rounds.
- If there are more than two goalkeepers, then they switch roles after every round.

Diving and Rolling Sideways

EXERCISE

GK1 stands in a standard goal, GK2 at the left post and the coach (C) directly in front of the goal. C has a ball and bounces it to the left of GK1, who deflects it to GK2, using the left hand. Then GK1 rolls over and jumps to the right for a second ball from C.

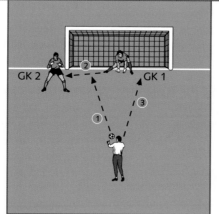

VARIATION

Instead of bouncing the ball, C passes on the ground.

FOCUS ON

- explosive lift with the takeoff leg (brief contact with the ground)
- accelerating directly toward the ball
- diving straight toward the ball
- catching the ball during the dive and securing it against the body

Jumping and Deflecting

EXERCISE

The goalkeeper stands in a standard goal, the coach (C) six yards directly in front of it. C has several balls and passes the first one on the ground toward the right corner of the goal. The goalkeeper dives for it and gets up. Then C throws the second ball over the goalkeeper, who dives for it and deflects it over the goal, using the right hand.

NOTE

- The goalkeeper thrusts the hand forward from the elbow to deflect the ball over the goal.

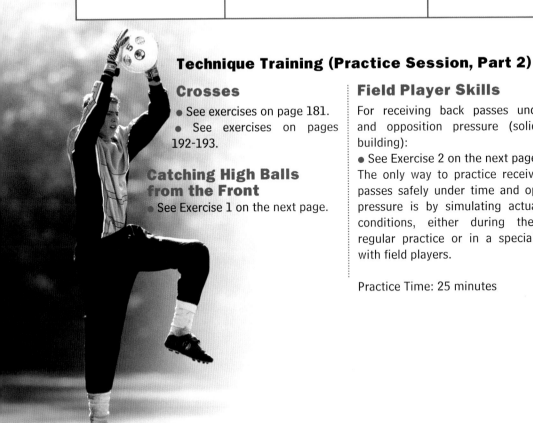

Technique Training (Practice Session, Part 2)

Crosses

- See exercises on page 181.
- See exercises on pages 192-193.

Catching High Balls from the Front

See Exercise 1 on the next page.

Field Player Skills

For receiving back passes under time and opposition pressure (solid attack building):

- See Exercise 2 on the next page.

The only way to practice receiving back passes safely under time and opposition pressure is by simulating actual match conditions, either during the team's regular practice or in a special session with field players.

Practice Time: 25 minutes

Motivational Exercises on the Goal

EXERCISE 1

The goalkeeper stands in a standard goal; the coach (C) has several balls and stands 20 yards in front of it. To C's left and right are two goals: a five-yard-wide goal with goalkeeper, 40 yards away (Goal 1) and another small goal with goalkeeper 30 yards away (Goal 2). At C's signal, the goalkeeper does a forward roll and catches a high ball from C. During the roll, the coach calls out a goal number, and then the goalkeeper shoots at that goal: either a drop-kick at Goal 1 or a throw at Goal 2.

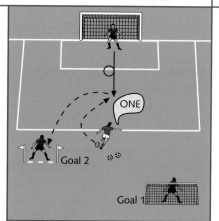

FOCUS ON

- throw: keeping the hand on the ball and, more importantly, behind it as long as possible
- drop-kick: adjusting the position of the torso depending on whether the kick is to be high, low or on the ground

NOTE

These two motivational exercises, combined, should last about 20 minutes.

EXERCISE 2

Two standard goals with goalkeepers (GK1 and GK2) stand facing each other, 20 yards apart. GK3 stands 20 yards behind the second goal and kicks precisely to GK1, who receives the ball like a back pass and passes it to GK2. Then GK2 tries to score on GK1's goal with a direct instep shot.

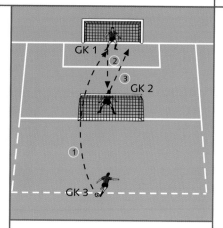

NOTE

- Goalkeepers switch positions after several rounds.

VARIATION

GK3 drop-kicks (or throws) precisely to GK1, who also drop-kicks (or throws) to GK2. Then GK2 tries to score with the same technique (drop-kick or throw).

These two motivational exercises, combined, should last about 20 minutes.

Keeper's friends – the gloves

PERFORMANCE IS THE RULE

Soccer goalkeepers often own more than one pair of gloves. Some gloves are used for training and daily practice sessions. Others are worn strictly for match play. There are even gloves for varying weather and field conditions.

Goalkeeper gloves are a performance item. Critical to this is their ability to help a goalkeeper grip the ball. The quality of the glove palm can then be considered of ultimate importance in judging a glove to be more suitable for training, match play, wet weather, or the condition of the field.

Natural latex foam is the material generally used for the palms of soccer goalkeeper gloves. In addition to its useful tactile characteristics, latex foam behaves consistently during its lifespan. It Tends to wear, sometimes even after only a few uses. However, latex foam also continues to offer original performance levels, no matter how thin or worn it gets.

An expensive, high quality latex foam (German) glove might only last as long as lesser quality gloves in terms of palm wear, but may offer better contact adhesive qualities. (Admiral Flash glove offers superior German Wet-Grip palm latex for all-weather match performance.) Alternately, the latex foam palm of less expensive gloves may not offer superb gripping characteristics, but the often substantially lower price makes them more suitable for daily practice sessions. (Admiral Raider glove offers textured palm foam with good training performance and durability.) It is not uncommon for a player to go through a few pairs of practice quality gloves in a season. This is still a more reasonable situation than practicing and playing in the same pair of top-end match quality gloves, which can often cost as much as 4 times more.

FIT AND FORM

Additional to the qualities and performance levels of the palm material itself, gloves are

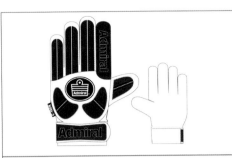

**ADMIRAL BOND
(K-77 WHITE/NAVY/BLACK)**

Super match glove. Exclusive C-tack process tactile palm. Embossed, printed backhand. Stay-cool breathable mesh pockets on the backhand. Elasticized wrist with Velcro closure. ERP: $50.00 Size: 7 to 11

**ADMIRAL MATCH
(K-80 BLACK/WHITE/GOLD)**

Match quality. Super soft 3.0mm latex foam palm. High compression embossed and printed backhand. Velcro closure. ERP: $40.00 Size: 6 to 11

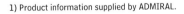

1) Product information supplied by ADMIRAL.

also designed to offer a variety of fit and comfort levels.

The latex foam for palms is typically available in a thickness of 2mm to 5mm. In an effort to decrease cost, thinner latex palm foams can be used in combination with secondary or backing layers of less expensive sponge foam. (Admiral Match glove offers 3mm latex foam palm with added padding of 3mm layer of sponge foam.) The feel of deluxe padding can be created without the expense of a single thick 5mm latex foam outer palm. It is a personal preference between goalkeepers whether or not thickly padded or thinner palms are desirable. For some, the extra padding offers a sense of extra protection when stopping the harder shots. For others, thick padding detracts from their 'feeling' the ball in their hands.

The shape or cut of gloves also affects the suitability of a goalkeeper glove. Less expensive gloves are usually given a full cut, with sidewalls on the fingers for plenty of movement. Upper end gloves, or those gloves sold for added style, can be given rounded, or 'barrel-cut' fingers which seem to surround the hand (Admiral Match glove), or have

backhands made with various materials (Admiral Bond Glove offers polyester mesh panels on the backhand for breathability). The combinations and design styles can be endless.

A GLOVE TO SUIT YOUR GAME

With all the choices of style, construction, performance and price, goalkeepers have several decisions. Typically, youth or recreational team goalkeepers will find that buying a single pair of reasonably priced gloves gives them a fair amount of performance and comfort without breaking the bank. Club select or travel team, high school and college level players may find themselves wanting 1-3 pairs of lower priced training gloves during the season and at least one pair of proper match quality gloves to back up their hard work and commitment in goal.

Youth players often do not warrant buying gloves over $30.00 in price. As they grow, and learn to look after their equipment, a player can consider to upgrade the glove quality to match their improving level of play. Most other players can't go wrong with middle of the road gloves, both in price and

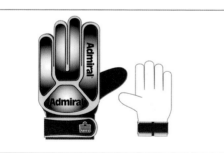

ADMIRAL RAIDER
(K-78 NAVY/GOLD/WHITE)

Durable training or youth match. Full cut glove, with textured 3.0mm latex foam palm. Full printing latex backhand. Velcro closure. ERP: $20.00 Size 6 to 11

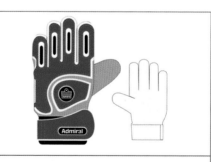

ADMIRAL FLASH
(K-81 METALLIC BLUE/GRAY/WHITE)

Premium glove. Superior German latex foam palm and wrist. Embossed and printed logos. Unique Tecno-Star synthetic leather backhand. Elastic band wrist with Velcro closure. ERP: $55.00 Size: 8 to 11

quality. A season's use, often including many practice sessions, is a reasonable demand on most pairs of gloves. The difficulty with goalkeeper gloves is that most choices are made by color and design. Bright colors, cool graphics or unusual materials often make the sale before considerations of expected performance or durability.

PROTECTING YOUR INVESTMENT

As with many products, there are usually care instructions included in the packaging of goalkeeper gloves. These suggestions are offered to help a player get the most out of his or her purchase. Although most players do not follow these suggested instructions to the letter very often, they are with some purpose.

Since direct sunlight is damaging to natural latex foam, properly store gloves between practice sessions or matches. It is often suggested to clean gloves after each (heavy) use by hand

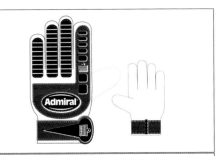

ADMIRAL ELLIPSE (K-79 RED/BLACK/WHITE)

Match quality glove. Super soft 3.0mm latex foam palm. High compression embossing and printed backhand. Velcro closure. ERP: $30.00 Size 6 to 11

washing them in warm water without detergent, squeezing out as much water as possible and allowing them to dry at room temperature. Goalkeepers need to be able to grip a soccer ball in wet and dry conditions. Latex foam rubber materials give goalkeeper gloves the desired gripping characteristics. However, foam rubber is a relatively soft material that cannot be guaranteed for durability. At least occasionally following the care instructions will help protect them from harmful elements and to extend their lifespan.

Kwik Back Rebounder

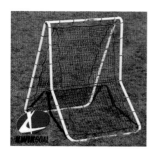

A goalkeeper needs a sharp mind and quick reflexes when the opposition sends in crosses and shots. With its unique "A-shaped" design, the Kwik Back Rebounder can give a complete workout to any 'keeper. Whether it is a low shot, or a high cross, the angles of this rebounder can be adjusted up to eight different ways, enabling a goalkeeper to work on all aspects of the game. These adjustments give the Kwik Back Rebounder the versatility to be used in different goalkeeper exercises, including the exercises introduced in this book.

The Rebound Net

Rebound nets are extremely useful training accessories – unfortunately, they are not exactly cheap. Still, a rebound net can be an excellent way to optimize your goalkeeper training program. If it is financially feasible to buy one for your club, then you should do so. Any good soccer equipment catalog should include rebound nets in its selection.

On all exercises involving the rebound net, you should keep a few points in mind:

• Goalkeepers need fixed orientation points at all times. During exercises, they should always stand in either standard goals or small ones, but never in the open field.

The speed and trajectory of the rebounding ball depend on several factors:

• thrower's distance from rebound net
• angle of approach (slope of rebound net)
• type of throw (overhand or underhand)
• force of throw
• special instructions from the coach.

General Technique Training

EXERCISE 1

Two goalkeepers practice together. Both stand in a seven-yard-wide goal, five yards in front of the rebound net. The front goalkeeper (GK1) throws a ball against the net and then runs behind GK2. GK2 tries to stop the rebounding ball with the chest and then catch it. Then GK2 throws the ball against the net and runs behind GK1, who stops with the chest and catches it, etc.

FOCUS ON
• technique training (field player skills)
• quickly pulling the ball in to the body

VARIATIONS

1. Stop the ball with the chest, bounce it up in the air with the knee and then catch it.
2. GK2 stands facing away from GK1. GK1 starts the exercise by giving a brief signal, simultaneously throwing the ball against the net. GK2 quickly turns around and stops the rebounding ball with the chest.
3. GK2 starts out lying face-down (or face-up, or in push-up position).

EXERCISE 2

Several goalkeepers practice together (each one has a ball). They stand in a seven-yard-wide goal, five yards in front of the rebound net. The first one throws a ball under-hand against the net, receives it, dribbles around the net (alternately to the left and to the right) and picks it up again.

FOCUS ON
- general technique training (field player skills)
- dribbling with the inside and outside of the foot, with both feet

VARIATIONS

1. Goalkeepers turn around quickly before receiving the ball (and stand farther away from the net).
2. Goalkeepers stand facing away from the net; at the coach's signal, they throw the ball between their legs against the net, turn around quickly and receive the ball.
3. The coach throws the ball; goalkeepers start from various starting positions (lying face-down or face-up, push-up position, etc.).

EXERCISE 3

The rebound net stands diagonally in front of the goalkeeper, 30 yards to the right of a small goal (five yards wide). The goalkeeper throws, receives the rebound-ing ball as quickly as possible and kicks a well-aimed ball on the ground through the small goal.

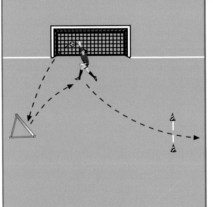

FOCUS ON
- general technique training (field player skills)
- focused, accurate receiving and passing

VARIATIONS

1. The goalkeeper shoots in the air at the small goal.
2. The goalkeeper volleys at the small goal.
3. The coach throws the ball; the goalkeeper starts from various starting positions (lying face-down or face-up, push-up position, etc.).

EXERCISE 4

The rebound net stands diagonally in front of GK1, who stands in a standard goal. 20 yards away stands GK2 in another standard goal. GK1 throws the ball against the net, receives it as quickly as possible, turns and tries to score on the other goal. If GK1 scores, the goalkeepers switch positions.

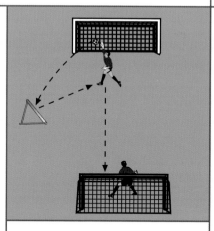

FOCUS ON
- general technique training (field player skills)
- accurate instep kicks at the goal

VARIATIONS
1. The goalkeepers play 1 v. 1 on the second goal.
2. Off the rebound, GK1 passes the ball directly to GK2. GK2 receives it and tries to score with a well-aimed instep shot.

EXERCISE 5

Two goalkeepers practice together. GK1 stands in a standard goal. GK2 has a ball and stands 16 yards in front of the goal and two yards behind the rebound net, facing away from GK1. GK2 throws the ball forcefully against the net and imme-diately turns to face GK1. GK1 receives the ball and passes precisely to GK2, who shoots off the first touch.

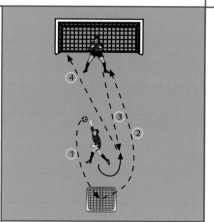

FOCUS ON
- general technique training (field player skills)
- receiving quickly
- passing accurately
- accurate instep kicks at the goal

VARIATIONS
1. GK1 passes the ball off the rebound with **one touch** to GK2.
2. The rebound net is placed diagonally (not directly) in front of GK2.

Goalkeeper Technique Exercises

You can use the rebound net to practice the following goalkeeper-specific techniques:

- assuming the basic position
- basic position technique
- throwing underhand
- throwing overhand
- picking up and catching ground balls and low balls from the front and side
- catching high balls from the side
- catching high balls from the front
- diving and rolling sideways on ground balls
- diving and jumping for balls on the ground and in the air, and rolling sideways
- jumping for high balls and falling backwards
- jumping and deflecting/punching

In the following pages, we present three basic exercises, which you can alter to fit your players' age and ability levels and your training objectives.

General Technique Training

EXERCISE 1

The goalkeeper has a ball and stands in a five-yard-wide goal, four or five yards in front of the rebound net. The slope and position of the net are changed during the exercise.

The goalkeeper throws the ball against the net (one-handed, underhand) so that it bounces straight back on the ground to be picked up.

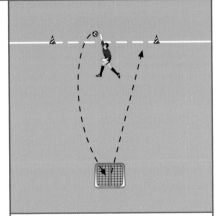

NOTE

- Goalkeeper should receive once with the right foot forward and once with the left foot forward.

VARIATIONS

1. The net is placed to one side of the goal, so that the goalkeeper has to receive ground balls from the side.
2. After throwing the ball, the goalkeeper turns around once completely.
3. The goalkeeper starts out lying face-down; the coach throws the ball against the net.

EXERCISE 2

Two goalkeepers line up in a goal and practice together; the front goalkeeper (GK1) has a ball. The rebound net is placed five yards in front of the goal. The slope and position of the net are changed during the exercise. GK1 throws the ball against the net (with both hands, overhand) so that the rebound is low in the air. Then GK1 quickly moves aside so that GK2 can catch the ball in front of the body. Then goalkeepers switch roles.

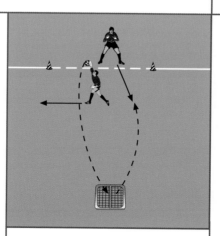

FOCUS ON

* practicing basic techniques: assuming the basic position, throwing overhand, catching high and low balls from the front and side, jumping and deflecting

VARIATIONS

1. GK1 waits until the last second to move aside, so that GK2 does not see the ball until it is almost too late.
2. GK2 stands directly beside GK1. GK1 throws the ball and stands still. GK2 quickly steps sideways in front of GK1 and catches the ball.
3. GK1 and GK2 stand back to back. At GK1's signal, GK2 (who is facing away from the goal) runs around GK1 as quickly as possible in order to catch a low ball from the front.

EXERCISE 3

The goalkeeper has a ball and stands in a standard goal. The coach (C) stands seven yards away at the rebound net, which faces the goalkeeper diagonally. The goalkeeper throws the ball against the net, either underhand with one hand or overhand with both. C "steers" the rebounding ball by shifting the net, so that the goalkeeper has to save a ground ball from the side.
After several rounds, move the net to the other side.

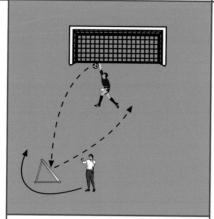

NOTE

* practicing basic techniques: assuming the basic position, diving and rolling sideways on ground balls, diving for balls on the ground and in the air and rolling sideways, and jumping and deflecting

VARIATIONS

1. C "steers" the rebounding ball so that the goalkeeper has to dive for a low or high ball in the air and can roll sideways afterwards.
2. The goalkeeper quickly turns around once completely before diving for the ball.
3. The goalkeeper stands facing away from the net, legs apart, and throws the ball between them against the net, then turns around quickly and catches a ground ball or low ball from the side ("steered" by C).